The Essential Commentaries for a Preacher's Library

Revised and Expanded

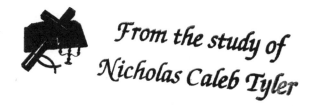

Derek W.H. Thomas
John W. Tweeddale

REFORMED ACADEMIC PRESS

FIRST PRES PRESS

1

The Essential Commentaries for a Preacher's Library

© 1996 Derek W. H. Thomas
© 2006 Derek W. H. Thomas and John W. Tweeddale

Printed in the United States of America

This book is a completely revised edition of *The Essential Comentaries for a Preacher's Library* first published in 1996 by Reformed Academic Press.

2nd Edition Published by:
First Presbyterian Church
1390 North State Street
Jackson, MS 39202
601.353.8316
www.fpcjackson.org

ISBN: 0-9777472-0-4

2

TABLE OF CONTENTS

PREFACE TO THE
REVISED AND EXPANDED EDITION

The great 19th century prince of preachers Charles Haddon Spurgeon opened his famous lectures on *Commenting and Commentaries* with this exhortation to all who preach the Word:

> In order to be able to expound the Scriptures, and as an aid to your pulpit studies, you will need to be familiar with the commentators: a glorious army, let me tell you, whose acquaintance will be your delight and profit. Of course, you are not such wiseacres as to think or say that you can expound Scripture without assistance from the works of divines and learned men who have laboured before you in the field of exposition...It seems odd, that certain men who talk so much of what the Holy Spirit reveals to themselves, should think so little of what he has revealed to others...The temptations of our times lie rather in empty pretensions to novelty of sentiment, than in a slavish following of accepted guides. A respectable acquaintance with the opinions of the giants of the past, might have saved many an erratic thinker from wild interpretations and outrageous inferences. Usually, we have found despisers of commentaries to be men who have no sort of acquaintance with them; in their case, it is the opposite of familiarity which has bred contempt.

Unfortunately, our day has seen even a less judicious use of solid commentaries, and the caliber of preaching has suffered for it. Though commentaries certainly don't make good preachers, they can serve as an invaluable aid to all who strive to preach biblically-based, prayer-saturated, Spirit-anointed, Christ-exalting, God-honoring sermons. For anyone, and especially the preacher, who seeks to rightly divide the word, a good commentary can be 'your delight and profit.' Therefore, we offer to you this commentary on commentaries.

Our aim in compiling this booklet is to provide you with a concise and up to date annotated bibliography of essential commentaries on each book of the Bible. Special attention is given to exegetical and expositional commentaries that may prove particularly helpful for sermon preparation. We hope our recommendations will serve as a reference tool for any individual who is a teacher and/or student of God's Word, but especially pastors, elders, seminary and college students, Sunday school teachers, and serious Bible students.

This booklet is a revision and expansion of *The Essential Commentaries for a Preacher's Library* by Derek Thomas which was published in 1996 by Reformed Academic Press (RAP). Since its original publication a host of new commentaries have emerged and are emerging – seemingly daily! So, like the first edition, this update is by no means an exhaustive list but an 'essential' list. Though the basic format has remained, several additions have been included.

First, minor changes to the original text have been updated (e.g. updating publication dates).

Second, select commentaries released since 1996 have been recommended and annotated.

Third, the section on *Essential Commentaries on the Whole Bible* has been expanded to include a short list of commentary sets available on CD-ROM. Some commentaries (e.g. older translations of Calvin's Commentaries) are available on the Internet, and readers should check, for example, the following site: http://www.ccel.org/index/classics.html.

Fourth, a section entitled *Essential Introductions to the Bible* has been introduced in order to provide assistance in understanding the various divisions and genres of the Bible. Like the commentaries, this list is not comprehensive but should point you in the right direction when preaching/teaching from a particular section of the Bible.

Fifth, an appendix entitled *Essential Systematic Theology Texts for a Preacher's Library* has been added out of the conviction that we not only need to know the parts of the Bible but also how those parts fit together. In other words, preachers should strive to be both exegetes and systematicians.

Finally, other more subtle revisions and additions are sprinkled throughout the text (e.g. a section on the *Ten Commandments*, the *Beatitudes*,*The Lord's Prayer,* etc.). For an explanation of the structure and format of this booklet, see the Notes to the First Edition.

We hope this reference aid will assist you in your study as you prepare to teach and preach God's Word. Ultimately, we want not just your love for commentaries to grow but your love for the Scriptures.

Derek W. H. Thomas
John W. Tweeddale
January 2006

NOTES TO THE FIRST EDITION

1.　In recommending some of these commentaries, I have kept in mind that a certain level of discernment is required, even from a seminary graduate! Thus, for example, in recommending Cranfield on Mark, Romans and Peter/Jude I have done so for the quality of his exegetical work. It must be remembered, however, that Cranfield (for example, in his analysis on Romans 11) is universalist in tone. Similarly, in recommending B. Childs on Exodus readers will need to discern critical analyses of the text. This need not necessarily detract from the value of the commentary as a whole, particularly for preachers, even if much more cautious notes would need to be sounded for lay readers. Ideally, there needs to be a recommendation for someone who has had a thorough theological grounding and another for someone who has not. Generally speaking, the latter are best sticking to the TOTC/TNTC series for a modern commentary and the older works cited for theological evaluation. I am assuming that a [seminary] graduate will be able to sift out the dross in some of the recommendations made.

2.　Few men will be in a position to purchase all of these commentaries at once (Gundry's commentary on Mark, for example, will set you back a small fortune, as will most exegetical commentaries on the Greek or Hebrew text). I have found that whenever I have begun an expository series on a given book, I have sought to purchase a number of commentaries on that book.

3.　The list is NOT exhaustive. I have included only a few commentaries on each book that I would regard as essential. Some are included because of invaluable exegetical help; others are helpful for sermon ideas and preparation. Preachers need all the help they can get, and a poor commentary (exegetically) can often provide useful ideas. Indeed, some of the books listed are not commentaries at all in the strict sense, but sermons. However, since the list is intended for preachers and to aid specifically in sermon preparation, I have included these also.

4.　There exists a leaning towards older, Puritan commentaries in the list. That is because of my belief that the Puritans got it right when it comes to application of the Word to the heart and soul. Following Jonathan Edwards' dictum: that theology/preaching (rightly understood) consists largely in the affections, reading the Puritans will help us get the balance right in what the aim of a sermon is all about. My own method is to read the modern commentaries first to get the best of exegetical work and then to turn to the older works to get the best idea for fleshing out these exegetical ideas.

5.   In the case of some books (e.g. Genesis, Psalms, Gospels, Romans, etc.) I have included more than a few entries. This is because of my own belief in the seminal importance of these books. For example, every preacher should have as many commentaries on Romans as he can lay his hands on (or his bank balance will hold out to!). I think of Alexander Whyte who had a standing order with his Bookseller to let him see every book on Romans that was printed. Though, in Whyte's case, he would return it if he found the view of Romans 7:14-25 to be other than the *believer* distressed by his sin!

6.   I must also confess that a less than conservative commentary can often prove helpful in sermon preparation, but the need for discernment is so great that I would not be in favor of recommending any of them in a list of this kind. I'm thinking of the Jewish commentaries by Cassuto, and Roman Catholic contributions of Raymond Brown on John.

7.   **I have not included sets of commentaries in the individual recommendations, e.g. Calvin.** Calvin is essential reading for any preacher of any book, and some of his commentaries have never been equaled. Readers should take it for granted that Calvin should be consulted wherever possible.

ABBREVIATIONS

AOTC	Apollos Old Testament Commentary
BECNT	Baker Exegetical Commentary on the New Testament
BNTC	Black's New Testament Commentary
BoT/BT	Banner of Truth
BSC	Bible Student's Commentary
BST	Bible Speaks Today
B & H	Broadman & Holman
CFP	Christian Focus Publications
CUP	Cambridge University Press
EBC	Expositor's Bible Commentary
EBS	Encountering Biblical Studies
EP	Evangelical Press
EPSC	Evangelical Press Study Commentary
EPW	Evangelical Press of Wales
GSC	The Geneva Series of Commentaries
HOTC	Holman Old Testament Commentary
HNTC	Holman New Testament Commentary
IVP	InterVarsity Press
ITC	International Theological Commentary
IVPNT	InterVarsity Press New Testament Commentary Series
KK	Klock & Klock
n.d.	no date
o/p.	out of print
OTL	Old Testament Library
NAC	New American Commentary
NCB	New Century Bible
NIBC	New International Bible Commentary
NICC	New International Critical Commentary
NICOT	New International Commentary on the Old Testament
NICNT	New International Commentary on the New Testament
NIGTC	New International Greek Testament Commentary

NIVAC	The NIV Application Commentary
PNTC	Pillar New Testament Commentary
PWS	Preaching the Word Series
P & R	Presbyterian & Reformed Publishing
REC	Reformed Expository Commentary Series
SDG	Soli Deo Gloria
TNTC	Tyndale New Testament Commentaries
TOTC	Tyndale Old Testament Commentaries
TPC	The Preacher's Commentary
WBC	Word Biblical Commentary
WCS	Welwyn Commentary Series
WEC	Wycliffe Exegetical Commentary

ESSENTIAL COMMENTARIES ON THE WHOLE BIBLE

HANDBOOKS

Ryken, Leland, Philip Graham Ryken, Jim Wilhoit. *Ryken's Bible Handbook: A Guide to Reading and Studying the Bible*. Carol Steam, IL: Tyndale House, 2005.

Without doubt the best introductory volume to the Bible available today by world-class scholars. Every student of Scripture needs this close at hand.

Dever, Mark. *Promises Made: The Message of the Old Testament* Wheaton, IL : Crossway, 2006.

Dever, Mark. *Promises Kept: The Message of the New Testament* Wheaton, IL: Crossway, 2005.

Outstanding overviews of each book of the Bible in 2 magnificent volumes. Sell your shirt and buy volumes for anyone serious about wanting to know the Bible thoroughly.

CLASSICS

Calvin, John. *Calvin's Commentaries*. 22 Volumes. Grand Rapids: Baker, 2003.

"The Prince of expositors." Volumes are missing between Judges and Job, and he harmonized Exodus to Deuteronomy as well as the synoptic gospels. Nevertheless, this is where a seminary graduate should start.

Henry, Matthew. *Matthew Henry's Commentary on the Whole Bible.* 6 Volumes. Peabody: Hendrickson, 1991.

No library is complete without this set. George Whitefield read this commentary four times on his knees. It cost, then, a quarter of an average working man's annual salary! Available in several formats.

Oden, Thomas, ed. *Ancient Christian Commentary on Scripture.* Downers Grove: IVP. Leicester: IVP, 2001.

A projected 28 volume set. Each volume (so far 17 have been released) represents a collection of the best theological, spiritual, and pastoral insights of the Church Fathers. In a day when critical commentaries have dominated, preachers would do well to familiarize themselves with the hermeneutical and homiletical heritage of the Patristics – despite their tendency towards allegory.

Poole, Matthew. *A Commentary on the Holy Bible.* 3 Volumes. Carlisle: BoT, 1996. Edinburgh: BoT, 1996.

Spurgeon once said, "If I must have only one commentary, and had read Matthew Henry *[and might we add Calvin!]* as I have, I do not know but what I should choose Poole." Great for poignant application.

ONE VOLUME COMMENTARIES

Elwell, Walter A., ed. ***Baker Commentary on the Bible.*** Grand Rapids: Baker, 2000.

> *Good for ascertaining the broad scope of a text. Contributions by Dillard, Chamblin, Harrison, Knight, Martens, Moo, Noll, Schreiner, and VanGemeren should especially be considered. Based on the New International Version.*

Sproul, R. C., ed. ***The Reformation Study Bible.*** Orlando: Ligonier, 2005.

> *An outstanding group of reformed scholars contribute invaluable notes to this timely study Bible. If you are looking for a concise, one-stop resource for the historical, exegetical, and theological context and content of each book of the Bible, this is it! Includes the full text of the English Standard Version.*

Wenham, G. J., J. A. Motyer, D. A. Carson, R. T. France, eds. ***New Bible Commentary: 21ˢᵗ Century Edition.*** Downers Grove: IVP, 1994. Leicester: IVP, 1994.

> *Uneven, but some excellent contributions (esp. Ferguson, Motyer, Silva, Waltke).*

COMMENTARY SETS ON CD-ROM

Though searchable capabilities are a plus, having a book in hand is preferred. Besides, purchasing a set in its entirety is not always prudent – inevitably some volumes are better than others. Nevertheless, purchasing a set on CD-ROM may be a good investment – especially for those with limited space and resources to build an extensive library.

Gaebelein, Frank E., ed. **The Expositor's Bible Commentary 5.0 on CD-Rom.** Grand Rapids: Zondervan, 2003.

Evangelical, expository, and mostly even-handed.

Kistemaker, Simon and William Hendriksen. **New Testament Commentary on CD-Rom.** Grand Rapids: Baker, 2004.

See comments below on *Complete Commentaries on the New Testament (p.81).*

Metzger, Bruce M., David A. Hubbard, and Glenn W. Barker, eds. **Word Biblical Commentary on CD-Rom, 58 Volume Edition.** Nashville: Thomas Nelson, 2004.

Scholarly though at times overly critical.

Oden, Thomas C., ed. **Ancient Christian Commentary on Scripture Volume 1 on CD-Rom.** Downers Grove: IVP, 2005.

Ogilvie, Lloyd J., ed. **The Preacher's Commentary CD-Rom.** Nashville: Thomas Nelson, 2004.

Homiletical. Originally *The Communicator's Commentary.*

ESSENTIAL INTRODUCTIONS TO THE BIBLE

OLD TESTAMENT

Recommendation:

Hendriksen, William. *Bible Survey: A Treasury of Bible Information.* 4th ed. Grand Rapids: Baker, 1995.

If you must have only one introduction to the Bible, this is it.

Motyer, Alec. *The Story of the Old Testament.* Grand Rapids: Baker, 2001.

An invaluable resource. This book has it all: surveys, biblical references, background, theology, pictures, maps, diagrams, bibliographies, and more!

Consider:

Arnold, Bill T., and Bryan E. Beyer. *Encountering the Old Testament: A Christian Survey.* EBS. Grand Rapids: Baker, 1999.

Lots of pictures!

Crossley, Gareth. *The Old Testament: Explained and Applied.* Auburn: EP, 2003. Darlington: EP, 2003.

A fairly comprehensive overview from an evangelical, Christological perspective.

Currid, John D. *Ancient Egypt and the Old Testament.* Grand Rapids: Baker, 1997.

Explores the Egyptian background to the Pentateuch, historical books, wisdom literature, and Israelite prophecy.

Dillard, Raymond B. and Tremper Longman III. *An Introduction to the Old Testament.* Grand Rapids: Zondervan, 1994.

Not as helpful as the New Testament counterpart by Carson and Moo but is more up to date than Hendriksen and Harrison.

Dumbrell, William J. *The Faith of Israel: Its Expression in the Books of the Old Testament.* 2nd ed. Grand Rapids: Baker, 2002.

Concise and thematic survey. Good for a quick overview of a book.

Harrison, Roland K. *Introduction to the Old Testament.* Peabody: Hendrickson, 2004.

A standard text. Includes an introduction to the Apocrypha.

Walton, John H., Victor H. Matthews, & Mark W. Chavalas. *The IVP Bible Background Commentary: Old Testament.* Downers Grove: IVP, 2000.

Cultural background for most passages in the OT.

Young, Edward J. *An Introduction to the Old Testament.* Grand Rapids: Eerdmans, 1970. o/p.

An older work but still worth referencing.

To be considered for sermon preparation:

Ellsworth, Roger. *The Bible Book by Book.* The Guide. Auburn: EP, 2002. Darlington: EP, 2002.

> *Short studies on each book of the bible. Meant for personal or group study.*

Fee, Gordon D., and Douglas Stuart. *How to Read the Bible for All Its Worth.* 3rd ed. Grand Rapids: Zondervan, 2003.

> *See chapters 9-12 on 'Laws,' 'Prophets,' 'Psalms,' and 'Wisdom.'*

PENTATEUCH

Recommendation:

Alexander, T. Desmond. *From Paradise to the Promised Land: An Introduction to the Main Themes of the Pentateuch.* 2nd ed. Grand Rapids: Baker, 2002.

> *Excellent for grasping broad biblical-theological themes despite the occasional passing reference to a 'received text.' Provides a comprehensive bibliography.*

Consider:

Alexander, T. Desmond and David W. Barker, eds. *Dictionary of the Old Testament Pentateuch.* Downers Grove: IVP, 2003. Leicester: IVP, 2003.

> *Simple, straightforward, scholarly articles.*

Allis, O. T. *God Spoke by Moses: An Exposition of the Pentateuch.* Phillipsburg: P & R, 1989.

A helpful overview of the books of Moses.

Hamilton, Victor P. *Handbook on the Pentateuch.* 2nd ed. Grand Rapids: Baker, 2005.

A chapter by chapter critical synopsis.

To be considered for sermon preparation:

Ainsworth, H. *Annotations on the Pentateuch.* 2 Volumes. Pittsburgh: SDG, 1991.

Verse by verse notes by this early 17th century English nonconformist. Includes the Psalms and Song of Solomon.

Roberts, Linleigh J. *Know your God: The Doctrine of God in the Pentateuch.* Webster: EP, 2005. Darlington: EP, 2005.

HISTORICAL BOOKS

Recommendation:

Hamilton, Victor P. *Handbook on the Historical Books.* Grand Rapids: Baker, 2001.

Inductively works through Joshua-Esther in order to highlight the structure and content of each book. Provides a comprehensive bibliography. Nicely compliments Howard, who provides more background info.

19

Howard Jr., David. *An Introduction to the Old Testament Historical Books.* Chicago: Moody, 1993.

Introduces key facts and figures; deductively summarizes each book (e.g. authorship, date, purpose, outline, theology of book, etc.). His introductory essay on historical narrative is insightful but his treatment of the question of 'deuteronomistic history' in relation to the historical books, though critical of M. Noth, should be read with care.

Consider:

Bright, John. *A History of Israel.* 4th ed. Louisville: Westminster, 2000.

A classic text. Not exactly evangelical theologically but fairly conservative historically. Should be on your shelf.

WISDOM & POETIC BOOKS

Recommendation:

No recommendation for one comprehensive introduction. See the selections below under To be considered for sermon preparation *for assistance with particular books.*

Consider:

Berry, Donald K. *An Introduction to Wisdom and Poetry in the Old Testament.* Nashville: B & H, 1999.

Good for the history of interpretation but not as helpful on background information.

Bolluck, C. Hassell. *An Introduction to the Old Testament Poetic Books.* Chicago: Moody, 1988.

Ryken, Leland, James C. Wilhoit, Tremper Longman III. *Dictionary of Biblical Imagery.* Downers Grove: IVP, 1998. Leicester: IVP, 1998.

Though not limited to the poetic books, there is a wealth of information to aid the preacher in interpreting poetic literature.

To be considered for sermon preparation:

Futato, Mark D. *Transformed by Praise: The Purpose and Message of the Psalms.* Phillipsburg: P & R, 2002.

Goldsworthy, Graeme. *Gospel and Wisdom.* The Goldsworthy Trilogy. Carlisle, UK: Paternoster, 2000.

Sets wisdom literature in its biblical-theological context.

Kidner, Derek. *An Introduction to Wisdom Literature: The Wisdom of Proverbs, Job & Ecclesiastes.* Downers Grove: IVP, 1985. Leicester: IVP, 1985.

Longman, Tremper III. *How to Read the Psalms.* Downers Grove: IVP, 1988. Leicester: IVP, 1988.

An essential read before trying to expound a psalm! Check for Psalms 98, 69, and 30.

Longman, Tremper III. *How to Read Proverbs.* Downers Grove: IVP, 2002. Leicester: IVP, 2002.

Rongen, G. van. *Be Wise! An Introduction to the Books of Proverbs.* Kelmscott, Western Australia: Pro Ecclesia Publishers, 1988. o/p.

Travers, Michael E. *Encountering God in the Psalms.* Grand Rapids: Kregel, 2003.

Powerful, perceptive, and pastoral. As a literature scholar, the author breathes energy and new life into the Psalms from an understanding of their genre.

PROPHETIC BOOKS

Recommendation:

Robertson, O. Palmer. *The Christ of the Prophets.* Phillipsburg: P & R, 2004.

The much anticipated sequel to his superb The Christ of the Covenants. This tour de force opens a window on the Old Testament prophets that sheds more than just light; it radiates a passion for their study and proclamation.

VanGemeren, Willem A. *Interpreting the Prophetic Word: An Introduction to the Prophetic Literature of the Old Testament.* Grand Rapids: Zondervan, 1990.

A solid text. Has a firm grasp of redemptive-history and covenant theology.

Consider:

Hassell, Bullock C. *An Introduction to the Old Testament Prophetic Books.* Chicago: Moody, 1986.

Williams, Michael J. *The Prophet and His Message.* Phillipsburg: P&R, 2003.

Young, Edward J. *My Servants the Prophets.* Eugene, OR: Wipf and Stock, 2001.

INTRODUCTION TO THE NEW TESTAMENT

Recommendation:

Carson, D. A., and Douglas J. Moo. *An Introduction to the New Testament.* 2nd ed. Grand Rapids: Zondervan, 2005.

> *A superb reference. This must be on your shelf and should be consulted before every sermon series. Also includes a helpful section on the New Perspective on Paul.*

Hendriksen, William. *Bible Survey: A Treasury of Bible Information.* 4th ed. Grand Rapids: Baker, 1995.

> See *Introduction to the Old Testament* above.

Stott, John. *The Story of the New Testament.* Grand Rapids: Baker, 2001.

> *An invaluable resource. This book has it all: surveys, biblical references, background, theology, pictures, maps, diagrams, bibliographies, and more!*

Consider:

Bruce, F. F. *New Testament History.* New York: Doubleday, 1980.

Helpful for understanding the backdrop to the New Testament.

Elwell, Walter A. and Robert W. Yarbrough. *Encountering the New Testament: A Historical and Theological Survey.* EBS. Grand Rapids: Baker, 1998.

Lots of pictures!

Evans, Craig A., and Stanley E. Porter. *Dictionary of New Testament Background.* Downers Grove: IVP, 2000. Leicester: IVP, 2000.

Short, straightforward, scholarly articles.

Guthrie, Donald. *New Testament Introduction.* Downers Grove: IVP, 1970.

Standard, trustworthy.

Keener, Craig S. *The IVP Bible Background Commentary: New Testament.* Downers Grove: IVP, 1993.

Cultural background for most passages in the New Testament.

Machen, J. Gresham. *The New Testament: An Introduction to its Literature and History.* Carlisle: BoT, 1976. Edinburgh: BoT, 1976.

Old but good; dated but reliable.

Ryken, Leland. *Words of Life: A Literary Introduction to the New Testament.* Grand Rapids: 1987.

Insightful. Well done literary criticism.

To be considered for sermon preparation:

Ellsworth, Roger. *The Bible Book by Book.* The Guide. Auburn: EP, 2002. Darlington: EP, 2002.

Short studies on each book of the bible. Meant for personal or group study.

Fee, Gordon D., and Douglas Stuart. *How to Read the Bible for All Its Worth.* 3rd ed. Grand Rapids: Zondervan, 2003.

> *See chapters 3-4 on the Epistles, 6 on Acts, 7-8 on the Gospels and Parables, and 13 on Revelation.*

Jeffery, Peter. *Stepping-Stones: A New Testament Guide for Beginners.* Carlisle: BoT, 1991. Edinburgh: BoT, 1991.

> *Written with lay teachers and young Christians in mind. Presents the background, structure, and content of New Testament in a simple and brief way.*

GOSPELS

Recommendation:

Block, Darell L. *Jesus according to Scripture: Restoring the Portrait from the Gospels.* Grand Rapids: Baker, 2002.

Blomberg, Craig. *Jesus and the Gospels.* Nashville: B & H, 1997.

Consider:

Bridge, Donald. *Why Four Gospels?* Ross-shire: CFP, 1996.

Bridge, Donald. *Jesus, the Man and his Message.* Ross-shire: CFP, 1995.

Green, Joel B., Scot McKnight, I. Howard Marshall. *Dictionary of Jesus and the Gospels.* Downers Grove: IVP, 1992. Leicester: IVP, 1992.

Reymond, Robert L. *Jesus: Divine Messiah.* Ross-shire: CFP, 2003.

Parables:

Blomberg, Craig L. *Interpreting the Parables.* Downers Grove: IVP, 1990. Leicester: IVP, 1990.

Blomberg, Craig L. *Preaching the Parables.* Grand Rapids: Baker, 2004.

Boice, James Montgomery. *The Parables of Jesus.* Chicago: Moody, 1983.

Jeremias, Joachim. *Rediscovering the Parables.* 2nd ed. Upper Saddle River, NJ: Prentice Hall, 1972.

Kistemaker, Simon. *The Parables of Jesus.* Grand Rapids: Baker, 2002.

Wenham, David. *The Parables of Jesus: Pictures of Revolution.* Downers Grove: IVP,   1989. Leicester: IVP, 1989.

PAULINE EPISTLES

Recommendation:

Ridderbos, Herman. *Paul: An Outline of His Theology.* Grand Rapids: Eerdmans, 1975.

Schreiner, Thomas R. *Paul: Apostle of God's Glory in Christ.* Downers Grove: IVP, 2001. Leicester: IVP, 2001.

See entry for his commentary on Romans below.

Consider:

Bruce, F. F. *Paul: An Apostle of the Heart Set Free.* Grand Rapids: Eerdmans, 1977.

Chamblin, J. Knox. *Paul and the Self: Apostolic Teaching for Personal Wholeness.* Grand Rapids: Baker, 1993.

Hawthorne, Gerald F., Ralph P. Martin, Daniel G. Reid. *Dictionary of Paul and His Letters.* Downers Grove: IVP, 1993.

Reymond, Robert L. *Paul: Missionary Theologian.* Ross-shire: CFP, 2000.

New Perspective(s) on Paul:

Given the current interest in the works of E. P. Sanders, James Dunn, and N. T. Wright, below are a few books surveying the New Perspectives on Paul.

Recommendation:

Duncan, J. Ligon. *Misunderstanding Paul?* Wheaton: Crossway, 2006.

A careful and concise introduction.

Waters, Guy Prentiss. *Justification and the New Perspectives on Paul: A Review and a Response.* Phillipsburg: P & R, 2004.

An outstanding analysis and critique. This is where you should start.

Westerholm, Stephen. *Perspectives Old and New on Paul: The "Lutheran" Paul and His Critics.* Grand Rapids: Eerdmans, 2004.

Most comprehensive one volume evaluation.

Consider:

Carson, D. A., Peter T. O'Brien, Mark A. Seifrid, eds. *Justification and Variegated Nomism.* Volume 1 – The Complexities of Second Temple Judaism. Grand Rapids: Baker, 2001.

Carson, D. A., Peter T. O'Brien, Mark A. Seifrid, eds. *Justification and Variegated Nomism.* Volume 2 – The Paradoxes of Paul. Grand Rapids: Baker, 2004.

Heavy reading. You may want to start with volume 2 which deals exclusively with the immediate issues related to the New Perspective.

Carson, D. A., and Douglas J. Moo. *An Introduction to the New Testament.* 2nd ed. Grand Rapids: Zondervan, 2005.

See comments above on Introduction to the New Testament.

GENERAL EPISTLES

Consider:

Martin, Ralph P., and Peter H. Davids. *Dictionary of the Later New Testament & Its Developments.* Downers Grove: IVP, 1997. Leicester: IVP, 1997.

ESSENTIAL COMMENTARIES ON THE OLD TESTAMENT

COMPLETE COMMENTARY ON THE OLD TESTAMENT

Keil, C. F., and F. Delitzsch. *Commentary on the Old Testament*. 10 Volumes. Updated ed. Peabody: Hendrickson, 1996.

A standard 19th century work by orthodox Lutheran scholars. A knowledge of Hebrew, Greek, and occasionally Latin will help but is not needed.

GENESIS

Recommendation:

Currid, John D. *A Study Commentary on Genesis. Volume 1: Genesis 1:1-25:18*. EPSC. Webster, New York: EP, 2003. Darlington: EP, 2003.

Currid, John D. *A Study Commentary on Genesis. Volume 2: Genesis 25:19-50:26*. EPSC. Webster, New York: EP, 2003. Darlington: EP, 2003.

Easy to read yet biblically robust expositions that seek to bridge the gap between technical and popular commentaries. Upholds a literal, six-day creation account and provides a helpful introduction to 'seed-theology.'

Wenham, Gordon J. *Genesis 1-15*. WBC. Waco: Word, 1987.

Wenham, Gordon J. *Genesis 16-50.* WBC. Waco: Word, 1994.

It is difficult to imagine a less user-friendly layout than the Word Biblical Commentary Series. The series is uneven and occasionally goes overboard in literary/source criticism. But at least one up-to-date, critical commentary on Genesis should be on our shelves, and this is about the best. Maintains a literary view of Genesis 1.

Consider:

Aalders, G. Ch. *Genesis, Volume I & II.* BSC. Grand Rapids: Zondervan, 1981. o/p.

English translation of the Dutch Korte Verklaring. Recommended by Simon Kistemaker.

Atkinson, David. *The Message of Genesis 1-11.* BST. Downers Grove: IVP, 1990. Leicester: IVP, 1990.

Baldwin, Joyce G. *The Message of Genesis 12-50.* BST. Downers Grove: IVP, 1986. Leicester: IVP, 1986.

Candlish, R. S. *Exposition of Genesis.* Lafayette: Sovereign Grace Publishers, 2001.

Hamilton, Victor P. *The Book of Genesis: Chapters 1-17.* NICOT. Grand Rapids: Eerdmans, 1990.

Hamilton, Victor P. *The Book of Genesis: Chapters 18-50.* NICOT. Grand Rapids: Eerdmans, 1995.

At best is ambiguous regarding Mosaic authorship and supports a literary interpretation of Genesis 1. Does provide an extensive, but now dated, bibliography.

Kidner, Derek. *Genesis: An Introduction and Commentary.* TOTC. Downers Grove: IVP, 1981. London: IVP, 1981.

Matthews, Kenneth A. *Genesis 1-11:26*. NAC. Nashville: B & H, 1996.

Matthews, Kenneth A. *Genesis 11:27-50:26*. NAC. Nashville: B & H, 2005.

> *Supports Mosaic authorship and maintains a non-literal view of creation.*

Ross, Allen P. *Creation & Blessing: A Guide to the Study and Exposition of Genesis*. Grand Rapids: Baker, 1998.

> *Strongly advocates Mosaic authorship and six-day creation. Technically not a commentary but a handy tool for better understanding the text.*

Waltke, Bruce K., and Cathi J. Fredericks. *Genesis: A Commentary*. Grand Rapids: Zondervan, 2001.

> *Literary framework.*

Books to be considered for sermon preparation:

Boice, James M. *Genesis*. An Expositional Commentary. 3 Volumes. Grand Rapids: Baker, 1998.

Duiguid, Iain M. *Living in the Gap Between Promise and Reality: The Gospel According to Abraham*. Phillipsburg: P & R, 2002.

Duiguid, Iain M. *Living in the Grip of Relentless Grace: The Gospel in the Lives of Isaac & Jacob*. Phillipsburg: P & R, 2002.

> *Short, Christ-centered studies on Genesis 11:27-25:18 and 25:19-35:29.*

Eveson, Philip H. *The Book of Origins: Genesis Simply Explained*. WCS. Darlington: EP, 2001.
Six-day creation.

Godfrey, W. Robert. *God's Pattern for Creation: A Covenantal Reading of Genesis 1.* Phillipsburg: P&R, 2003.

Framework. Influence of Meredith Kline is clearly evident.

Hughes, R. Kent. *Genesis: Beginning and Blessing.* PWS. Wheaton, Crossway, 2004.

A helpful homiletical commentary. Holds an analogical view of creation.

Jackman, David. *Abraham: Believing God in an Alien World.* Leicester: IVP, 1987.

Jensen, Phillip, and Tony Payne. *Beginnings: Eden and Beyond: Genesis 1-11.* Wheaton: Crossway, 1999.

Kendall, R. T. *God Meant it for Good: The Story of Joseph Speaks to Us Today.* Eastbourne: Kingsway, 1986.

This is early Kendall before his views changed.

Lane, Denis. *A Man and His God.* WCS. Welwyn: EP, 1981.

Law, Henry. *The Gospel in Genesis.* Carlisle: BT, 1993. Edinburgh: BT, 1993.

Lawson, George. *Lectures on the History of Joseph.* London: BT, 1972.

Longman III, Tremper. *How to Read Genesis.* Downers Grove: IVP, 2005.

MacMillan, J. Douglas. *Wrestling With God: Lessons from the Life of Jacob.* Bryntirion: EPW, 1991.

MacMillan was, perhaps, the best preacher in the Free Church of Scotland during the latter half of the 20th century. As a model of how to preach on historical chapters, this is essential reading.

Taylor, W. M. *Joseph, The Prime-Minister.* 1886. Grand Rapids: Baker, 1961.

Out of print, but if you can get hold of it – buy it!

Young, E. J. *Studies in Genesis One.* Phillipsburg: P & R, 1999.

Framework.

Young, E. J. *Genesis 3: A Devotional and Expository Study.* Edinburgh: BoT, 1966.

For further study on creation, consider the following:

Hagopian, David G. ed. *The Genesis Debate: Three Views on the Days of Creation.* Mission Viejo, CA: Crux Press, 2001.

Ligon Duncan and David Hall present the 24-Hour view, Hugh Ross and Gleason Archer present the Day-Age view, and Lee Irons with Meredith Kline present the Framework view.

Pipa, Jr., Joseph A., and David W. Hall, eds. *Did God Create in Six Days?* Taylors, SC: Southern Presbyterian Press, 1999.

EXODUS

Recommendation:

Childs, Brevard S. *The Book of Exodus.* OTL. Philadelphia: Westminster, 1974.

> *Adopts a critical stance.*

Currid, John D. *A Study Commentary on Exodus. Volume 1: Chapters 1-18.* EPSC. Auburn, MA: EP, 2000. Darlington: EP, 2000.

Currid, John D. *A Study Commentary on Exodus. Volume 2: Chapters 19-40.* EPSC. Auburn, MA: EP, 2000. Darlington: EP, 2001.

> *In a refreshing way pays close attention to the text without getting bogged down in critical discussions. Helpful section on the Decalogue in volume 2.*

Motyer, J. Alec. *The Message of Exodus.* BST. Downers Grove: IVP, 2005. Leicester: IVP, 2005.

> *A superb commentary. Scholarly, simple, and sensible. While focusing on the text his footnotes will point eager students in the right direction for further study.*

Consider:

Cole, Alan. *Exodus: An Introduction and Commentary.* TOTC. Downers Grove: IVP, 1973. Leicester: IVP, 1973.

Davis, John J. *Moses and the Gods of Egypt: Studies in Exodus.* 2nd ed. Grand Rapids:Baker, 1986.

Enns, Peter. *Exodus.* NIVAC. Grand Rapids: Zondervan, 2000.

Gispen, W. H. *Exodus.* BSC. Grand Rapids: Zondervan, 1982. o/p.

Kaiser, Jr., Walter C. *Exodus.* EBC. Grapd Rapids: Zondervan, 1990.

Mackay, John L. *Exodus.* A Mentor Commentary. Ross-shire: CFP, 2001.

Good exposition; good application.

Books to be considered for sermon preparation:

Bentley, Michael. *Traveling Homeward: Exodus Simply Explained.* WCS. Auburn, MA: EP, 1999. Darlington: EP, 1999.

Bush, George. *Notes on Exodus.* 2 Volumes. Minneapolis: KK, 1976.

George Bush, b. 1796, graduate of Princeton in 1824 and later pastor of a Presbyterian Church in Indianapolis. In 1831 he was elected professor of Hebrew and Oriental Literature at the University of New York.

Dray, Stephen. *Exodus.* Crossway Bible Guides. Nottingham: Crossway, 1993. o/p.

Ferguson, Sinclair B. *A Heart for God.* Carlisle: BoT, 1990. Edinburgh: BoT, 1987.

Chapter 5, 'The Ever Present One' provides a preacher with a model of how to exegete and preach Exodus 3 – one of the foundational chapters in Scripture.

Law, Henry. *The Gospel in Exodus.* London: BoT, 1967.

Ryken, Philip G. *Exodus: Saved for God's Glory.* PWS. Wheaton: Crossway, 2005.

For further study on the Ten Commandments, consider the following:

Douma, J. *The Ten Commandments: Manual for the Christian Life.* Trans. Nelson D. Kloosterman. Phillipsburg: P & R, 1996.

Ridgeley, Thomas. *Commentary on the Larger Catechism.* Volume 2. 1855. Edmonton: Still Waters Revival, 1993.

Ryken, Philip Graham. *Written in Stone: The Ten Commandments and Today's Moral Crisis.* Wheaton: Crossway, 2003.

Vincent, Thomas. *The Shorter Catechism Explained from Scripture.* Carlisle: BoT, 1980. Edinburgh: BoT, 1980.

Vos, Johannes G. *The Westminster Larger Catechism: A Commentary.* Ed. G. I. Williamson. Phillipsburg: P & R, 2002.

Watson, Thomas. *The Ten Commandments.* Carlisle: BoT, 1996. Edinburgh: BoT, 1996.

Whyte, Alexander. *An Exposition on the The Shorter Catechism.* Ross-shire: CFP, 2004.

Williamson, G. I. *The Shorter Catechism.* Volume 2. Phillipsburg: P & R, 2003.

For further study on the Tabernacle, consider the following:

Gooding, D. W. *How to Teach the Tabernacle.* Everyday Publications, 1972. o/p.

Soltau, Henry W. *The Holy Vessels and Furniture of the Tabernacle.* Grand Rapids: Kregel, 1986.

Soltau, Henry W. *The Tabernacle, Priesthood, and the Offerings.* Grand Rapids: Kregel, 1990.

LEVITICUS

Recommendation:

Currid, John D. *A Study Commentary on Leviticus.* EPSC. Webster: EP, 2004. Darlington: EP, 2004.

Clearly and cogently presents Leviticus as a series of directories for public worship and establishes the importance of Leviticus for the NT. Especially helpful on the Holiness Code.

Tidball, Derek. *The Message of Leviticus.* BST. Downers Grove: IVP, 2005. Leicester: IVP, 2005.

Wenham, Gordon J. *The Book of Leviticus.* NICOT. Grand Rapids: Eerdmans, 1992.

Ambivalent regarding dating but exegesis of text is extremely useful.

Consider:

Bonar, Andrew. *Leviticus.* GSC. Carlisle: BT, 1979. Edinburgh: BT, 1979.

Typology at its best!

Harris, R. Laird. *Leviticus.* EBC. Grand Rapids: Zondervan, 1990.

Harrison, R. K. *Leviticus: An Introduction and Commentary.* TOTC. Downers Grove: IVP, 1980. Leicester: IVP, 1980.

Noordizij, A. *Leviticus.* BSC. Grand Rapids: Zondervan, 1982. o/p.

Rooker, Mark F. *Leviticus.* NAC. Nashville: B & H, 2000.

Ross, Allen P. *Holiness to the Lord: A Guide to the Exposition of the Book of Leviticus.* Grand Rapids: Baker, 2002.

NUMBERS

Recommendation:

Philip, James. *Numbers.* TPC. Nashville: Thomas Nelson, 2002.

Wenham, Gordon J. *Numbers: An Introduction and Commentary.*
TOTC. Downers Grove: IVP, 1981. Leicester: IVP, 1981.

Overall, a good, brief exposition of the text. While his introductory discussions are solid (esp. on typology), his discussion on the transmission of the text is at points muddied.

Consider:

Ashley, Timothy R. *The Book of Numbers.* NICOT. Grand Rapids: Eerdmans, 1993.

Brown, Raymond. *The Message of Numbers: Journey to the promised land.* BST. Downer Grove: IVP, 2002. Leicester: IVP, 2002.

Harrison, R. K. *Numbers.* WEC. Chicago: Moody, 1990.

Noordtzij, A. *Numbers.* BSC. Grand Rapids: Zondervan, 1983. o/p.

Books to be considered for sermon preparation:

Keddie, Gordon J. *According to Promise: The message of the book of Numbers.* WCS. Auburn: EP, 1993. Darlington: EP, 1993.

DEUTERONOMY

Recommendation:

Craigie, P. C. *The Book of Deuteronomy.* NICOT. Grand Rapids: Eerdmans, 1976.

Especially helpful on the role of the covenant in Deuteronomy.

Consider:

Brown, Raymond. *The Message of Deuteronomy.* BST. Downers Grove: IVP, 1993. Leicester: IVP, 1993.

Brown has an unfortunate remark about 'prophetic utterances,' p. 188, otherwise the commentary is helpful for preachers.

McConville, J. G. *Deuteronomy.* AOTC. Downers Grove: IVP, 2002. IVP: Leicester, 2002.

Rightly sees the notion of covenant as the regulating principle of Deuteronomy and astutely shows the importance of Deuteronomy for our understanding of the prophetic books. Waffles on dating and authorship.

Ridderbos, J. *Deuteronomy.* BSC. Grand Rapids: Zondervan, 1984. o/p.

Thompson, J. A. *Deuteronomy: An Introduction and Commentary.* TOTC. Downers Grove: IVP, 1981. London: IVP, 1981.

Books to be considered for sermon preparation:

Calvin, John. *Sermons on Deuteronomy.* Facsimile of 1583 Edition. Carlisle: BoT, 1987. Edinburgh: BoT, 1987.

Ferguson, Sinclair B. *A Heart for God.* Carlisle: BoT, 1987. Edinburgh: BoT, 1987.

> *Chapter 11, "Remember the Lord," is especially valuable as an example of how to preach Deuteronomy 8.*

JOSHUA

Recommendation:

Davis, Dale Ralph. *No Falling Words: Expositions of the Book of Joshua.* Focus on the Bible. Ross-shire: CFP, 2000.

> *Sets the standard for how to expound and apply historical narrative.*

Woudstra, Marten H. *The Book of Joshua.* NICOT. Grand Rapids: Eerdmans, 1991.

> *It is difficult to recommend a single commentary on Joshua, and this one is not as good as it could be.*

Consider:

Goslinga, J. *Joshua, Judges, Ruth.* BSC. Grand Rapids: Zondervan, 1986. o/p.

Huffman, Jr., John A. *Joshua.* TPC. Nashville: Thomas Nelson, 2002.

Books to be considered for sermon preparation:

Boice, James Montgomery. *Joshua: An Expositional Commentary.* Grand Rapids: Baker, 2005.

> *Not as deep a treatment as would be normal for Boice.*

Jeffrey, Peter. *Overcoming Life's Difficulties: Learning from the Book of Joshua.* Auburn: EP, 1999. Darlington: EP, 1999.

Pink, Arthur W. *Gleanings in Joshua.* Chicago: Moody, 1964.

Schaeffer, Francis A. *Joshua and the Flow of Biblical History.* The Complete Works of Francis A. Schaeffer. Volume 2. Wheaton: Crossway, 1985.

JUDGES

Recommendation:

Block, Daniel I. *Judges, Ruth.* NAC. Nashville: B & H, 1999.

Davis, Dale Ralph. *Judges: Such a Great Salvation.* Focus on the Bible. Ross-shire: CFP, 2000.

> *An exemplary "theo-centric exposition" – full of anecdotes and applications. Those looking for more background information, see Block.*

Consider:

Cundall, Arthur E. "Judges." *Judges and Ruth: An Introduction and Commentary.* TOTC. Downers Grove: IVP, 1981. Leicester: IVP, 1981.

Fausset, Andrew R. *A Critical and Expository Commentary on the Book of Judges.* GSC. Carlisle: BoT, 1999. Edinburgh: BoT, 1999.

Jackman, David. *Judges/Ruth.* TPC. Nashville: Thomas Nelson, 2002.

Wilcock, Michael. *The Message of Judges.* BST. Downers Grove: IVP, 1993. Leicester: IVP, 1993.

To be considered for sermon preparation:

Barber, Cyril J. *Judges: A Narrative of God's Power.* Neptune, NJ: Loizeaux Brothers, 1990. o/p.

Keddie, Gordon. *Even in Darkness: Studies in Judges and Ruth.* WCS. Welwyn: EP, 1993.

Phillips, W. Gary. *Judges, Ruth.* HOTC. Nashville: B & H, 2004.

Rogers, Richard. *A Commentary on Judges.* Facsimile of 1615 edition. Carlisle: BoT, 1991. Edinburgh: BoT, 1991.

RUTH

Recommendation:

Duguid, Iain M. *Esther and Ruth.* REC. Phillipsburg: P & R, 2005.

Look for this series to set the standard for reformed, expository commentaries.

Hubbard, Robert L. *The Book of Ruth.* NICOT. Grand Rapids: Eerdmans, 1988.

A substantial commentary in size and achievement.

Consider:

Atkinson, David. *The Wings of Refuge: The Message of Ruth.* BST. Downers Grove: IVP, 1983. Leicester: IVP, 1983.

Block, Daniel I. *Judges, Ruth.* NAC. Nashville: B & H, 1999.

Jackman, David. *Judges/Ruth.* TPC. Nashville: Thomas Nelson, 2002.

Morris, Leon. "Ruth." *Judges and Ruth: An Introduction and Commentary.* TOTC. Downers Grove: IVP, 1981. London: Tyndale Press, 1981.

To be considered for sermon preparation:

Ferguson, Sinclair B. *A Heart for God.* Carlisle: BoT, 1987. Edinburgh: BoT, 1987.

Chapter 9, "The Faithful Provider," is especially valuable as an example of how to preach Ruth 1.

Fortner, Donald S. *Discovering Christ in Ruth: The Kinsman Redeemer.* Auburn: EP, 1999. Darlington: EP, 1999.

Keddie, Gordon. *Even in Darkness: Studies in Judges and Ruth.* WCS. Welwyn: EP, 1993.

Luter, A. Boyd, and Barry C. Davis. *Ruth & Esther: God Behind the Seen.* Focus on the Bible. Ross-shire: CFP, 2003.

Phillips, W. Gary. *Judges, Ruth.* HOTC. Nashville: B & H, 2004.

1 & 2 SAMUEL

Recommendation:

Baldwin, Joyce. *1 & 2 Samuel: An Introduction and Commentary.* TOTC. Downers Grove: IVP, 1989. Leicester: IVP, 1989.

This is a brief commentary, but other commentaries, e.g. the two by Klein and Anderson in the Word Biblical Commentary Series, are heavily into text and literary criticism and have very little to help busy preachers.

Davis, Dale Ralph. *1 Samuel: Looking on the Heart.* Focus on the Bible. Ross-shire: CFP, 2003.

Davis, Dale Ralph. *2 Samuel: Out of Every Adversity.* Focus on the Bible. Ross-shire: CFP, 2004.

Deals ably with the text and doesn't get weighed down in critical matters.

Consider:

Bergen, Robert D. *1, 2 Samuel.* NAC. Nashville: B & H, 1996.

Evans, Mary J. *The Message of Samuel.* TBS. Downers Grove: IVP, 2004. Leicester: IVP, 2004.

Gordon, Robert P. *1 & 2 Samuel: A Commentary.* Grand Rapids: Zondervan, 1999.

To be considered for sermon preparation:

Briscoe, Stuart. *David: A Heart for God. Discover why the Lord delights in a transparent life.* Wheaton: Victor Books, 1984.

Calvin, John. *Sermons on 2 Samuel.* Carlisle: BoT, 1992. Edinburgh: BoT, 1992.

Ellsworth, Roger. *The Shepherd King: Learning from the Life of David.* Darlington: EP, 1998.

Keddie, Gordon J. *Dawn of a Kingdom: The Message of 1 Samuel.* WCS. Welwyn: EP, 1993.

Keddie, Gordon J. *Triumph of the King: The Message of 2 Samuel.* WCS. Welwyn: EP, 1993.

Pink, Arthur W. *The Life of David.* Grand Rapids: Baker, 1998.

Taylor, W. M. *David King of Israel: His Life and its Lessons.* London: Charles Burnett & Co., 1889. o/p.

Taylor's books are difficult to find, but always worth purchasing when obtainable. Other books by Taylor include: Joseph the Prime Minister, Daniel the Beloved, Elijah the Prophet, Peter the Apostle, and Paul the Missionary.

1 & 2 KINGS

Recommendation:

Davis, Dale Ralph. *The Wisdom and the Folly: An Exposition of the Book of First Kings.* Fearn: CFP, 2002.

Davis, Dale Ralph. *2 Kings: The Power and the Fury.* Focus on the Bible. Ross-shire: CFP, 2005.

A theological, expository commentary. See notes on Joshua.

Wiseman, Donald J. *1 & 2 Kings: An Introduction and Commentary.* TOTC. Downers Grove: IVP, 1993. Leicester: IVP, 1993.

> *Terse and to the point. Holds to single authorship.*

Consider:

Dilday, Russell H. *1, 2 Kings.* TPC. Nashville: Thomas Nelson, 2002.

House, Paul R. *1 & 2 Kings.* NAC. Nashville: B & H, 1998.

To be considered for sermon preparation:

Dillard, Raymond B. *Faith in the Face of Apostasy: The Gospel According to Elijah & Elisha.* Phillipsburg: P & R, 1999.

Ellsworth, Roger. *From Glory to Ruin: 1 Kings Simply Explained.* WCS. Auburn: EP, 2000. Darlington: EP, 2000.

Ellsworth, Roger. *Apostasy, Destruction and Hope: 2 Kings Simply Explained.* WCS. Auburn: EP, 2002. Darlington: EP, 2002.

Ellsworth, Roger. *Standing for God: The Story of Elijah.* Carlisle: BoT, 1994. Edinburgh: BoT, 1994.

Krummacher, F. W. *Elijah.* Grand Rapids: Kregel, 1993.

Krummacher, F. W. *Elisha.* Grand Rapids: Kregel, 1993.

Pierson, Lance. *Elijah: Standing for God in a Hostile World.* Leicester: IVP, 1991.

> *Somewhat racy and superficial in style, but has some useful ideas.*

Pink, Arthur W. *The Life of Elijah.* Carlisle: BoT, 1991. London: BT, 1963.

Pink, Arthur W. *Gleanings from Elisha: His Life and Miracles.* Chicago: Moody, 1999.

Stewart, Alexander. *The Prophet of Grace: An expositional and devotional study of the life of Elisha.* Edinburgh: Knox, 1993. o/p.

van Rongen, G. *Elisha the Prophet.* Kelmscott, Australia: Pro Ecclesia Publishers, 1988.

Exceptionally valuable from a Dutch, Reformed, Heidelberg tradition.

1 & 2 CHRONICLES

Recommendation:

Allen, Leslie C. *1, 2 Chronicles.* TPC. Nashville: Thomas Nelson, 2002.

Helpful tips for preaching.

Dillard, Raymond B. *2 Chronicles.* WBC. Nashville: Thomas Nelson, 1987.

Masterful exegesis. His interaction with Samuel-Kings and Chronicles is thorough; however, you may be left wanting for application of the text.

Pratt, Jr., Richard L. *1 and 2 Chronicles.* A Mentor Commentary. Ross-shire: CFP, 1998.

> *Excellent! Keeps the theology of the text central. Identifies 28-major biblical-theological motifs.*

Consider:

Selman, Martin J. *1 Chronicles: An Introduction and Commentary.* TOTC. Downers Grove: IVP, 1994. Leicester: IVP, 1994.

Selman, Martin J. *2 Chronicles: An Introduction and Commentary.* TOTC. Downers Grove: IVP, 1994. Leicester: IVP, 1994.

Wilcock, Michael. *The Message of Chronicles.* BST. Downers Grove: IVP, 1987. Leicester: IVP, 1987.

To be considered for sermon preparation:

Barber, Cyril J. *1 Chronicles: God's Faithfulness to the People of Judah.* Focus on the Bible. Ross-shire: CFP, 2004.

Barber, Cyril J. *2 Chronicles: God's Blessings of His Faithful People.* Focus on the Bible. Ross-shire: CFP, 2004.

Corduan, Winfried. *I & II Chronicles.* HOTC. Nashville: B & H, 2004.

Stewart, Andrew. *A Family Tree: 1 Chronicles Simply Explained.* WCS. Auburn: EP, 1997. Darlington: EP, 1997.

Stewart, Andrew. *A House of Prayer: The message of 2 Chronicles.* WCS. Auburn: EP, 2001. Darlington: EP, 2001.

EZRA & NEHEMIAH

Recommendation:

Fensham, F. Charles. *The Books of Ezra and Nehemiah.* NICOT. Grand Rapids: Eerdmans, 1994. A serious commentary; takes a traditional approach to dating, theology, etc.

Kidner, Derek. *Ezra and Nehemiah: An Introduction and Commentary.* TOTC. Downers Grove: IVP, 1981. London: IVP, 1981.

Succinct. Helpful appendices on historical matters.

Consider:

Brown, Raymond. *The Message of Nehemiah.* BST. Downers Grove: IVP, 1998. Leicester: IVP, 1998.

Williamson, H. G. M. *Ezra, Nehemiah.* WBC. Waco: Word, 1985.

To be considered for sermon preparation:

Boice, James M. *Nehemiah.* An Expositional Commentary. Grand Rapids: Baker, 2004.

Evers, Stan K. *Doing a Great Work: Ezra and Nehemiah Simply Explained.* WCS. Darlington: EP, 1996.

Packer, James I. *A Passion for Faithfulness: Wisdom from the Book of Nehemiah.* Wheaton: Crossway, 1995.

Philip, James. *Building for God.* Aberdeen: Didasko Press, n.d.

White, John. *Excellence in Leadership.* Downers Grove: IVP, 1986.

ESTHER

Recommendation:

Baldwin, Joyce G. *Esther: An Introduction and Commentary.* TOTC. Downers Grove: IVP, 1984. Leicester: IVP, 1984.

A short commentary; pays close attention to literary and historical aspects.

Duguid, Iain M. *Esther and Ruth.* REC. Phillipsburg: P & R, 2005.

See comments above on Ruth.

Consider:

Jobes, Karen H. *Esther.* NIVAC. Grand Rapids: Zondervan, 1999.

McConville, J. G. *Ezra, Nehemiah, and Esther.* Daily Study Bible. Philadelphia: Westminster, 1985.

To be considered for sermon preparation:

Bloomfield, Peter. *Esther.* The Guide. Auburn: EP, 2002. Darlington: EP:2002.

Carson, Alexander. *Confidence in God in Times of Danger.* Sterling, VA: G.A.M. Publication, n. d.

Very strongly Calvinistic, written by a Presbyterian, later Baptist minister in Northern Ireland. His line is the Providence of God.

Larson, Knute, and Kathy Dahlen. *Ezra, Nehemiah, Esther.* HOTC. Nashville, B & H, 2005.

Prime, Derek. *Unspoken lessons about the unseen God: Esther Simply Explained.* WCS. Auburn: EP, 2001. Darlington: EP, 2001.

Still, William. *Sermons on the Book of Esther.* Aberdeen: Didasko Press, n.d.

> *Still takes it as being the battle of the ages between God and the Devil, to cut Christ off before he is born.*

JOB

Recommendation:

Anderson, Francis. I. *Job: An Introduction and Commentary.* TOTC. Downers Grove: IVP, 1981. Leicester: IVP, 1981.

Clines, David J. A. *Job 1-20.* WBC. Waco: Word, 1989.

> *This is the most comprehensive commentary on Job 1-20 available. Volumes 2 (Job 21-37) and 3 (Job 38-42 plus 200 pg index!!!) are still pending. Clines deserves to be read thoroughly, though there are times when he is irritatingly defensive on Christological implications in the 'big' texts in Job. For a summary, consult his commentary in the New Bible Commentary, 21st Century Edition, pp. 459-484.*

Consider:

Atkinson, David. *The Message of Job.* BST. Downers Grove: IVP, 1991. Leicester: IVP, 1991.

Durham, James. *Lectures on Job.* Dallas: Naphtali Press, 1995.

> *This is a 'must' for anyone wanting a Puritan view of Job.*

Hartley, John E. *The Book of Job.* NICOT. Grand Rapids: Eerdmans, 1991.

McKenna, David L. *Job.* TPC. Nashville: Thomas Nelson, 2002.

To be considered for sermon preparation:

Bloomfield, Peter. *Job.* The Guide. Darlington: EP, 2003.

Caryl, Joseph. *An Exposition with Practical Observations on Job.* 12 Volumes. Grand Rapids: Dust & Ashes Publications and Reformed Heritage Books, 2001.

Caryl (d. 1673) preached over 400 sermons spanning an unprecedented twenty-four years on this one book. These sermons are worthy of reading for their exegetical insights, thoughtful applications, and pastoral sensitivity.

Calvin, John. *Sermons on Job.* Facsimile of 1574 Edition. Carlisle: BoT, 1993. Edinburgh: BoT, 1993.

Fyall, Robert. *How God Treats His Friends.* Ross-shire: CFP, 1995.

For a more in-depth biblical-theological study of Job, see the author's revision of his dissertation, Robert S. Fyall, Now my eyes have seen you: Images of creation and evil in the book of Job, New Studies in Biblical Theology (Downers Grove: IVP, 2002).

Green, William Henry. *Conflict and Triumph: The Argument of the Book of Job Unfolded.* Carlisle: BoT, 1999. Edinburgh: BoT, 1999.

Green (d. 1900) was chair of Biblical and Oriental Literature at Princeton Theological Seminary for nearly fifty years.

Littleton, Mark R. *When God Seems Far Away: Biblical Insights for Common Depression.* Wheaton: Shaw, 1987.

Philip, George M. *Lord, from the Depths I Cry: A Study in the Book of Job.* Glasgow: Nicholas Gray Publishing, 1986.

Thomas, Derek. *When the Storm Breaks: Job Simply Explained.* WCS. Darlington: EP, 1995.

Thomas, Derek. *Mining for Wisdom: 28 Daily Readings from Job.* Auburn: EP, 2002. Darlington: EP, 2002.

Thomas, Derek. *Calvin's Teaching on Job: Proclaiming the Incomprehensible God.* Ross-shire: CFP, 2004.

Tinker, Melvin. *Why Do Bad Things Happen to Good People?* Ross-shire: CFP, 2004.

PSALMS

Recommendation:

Allen, Leslie A. *Psalms 101-150.* WBC. Waco: Word, 2002.

This commentary has serious weaknesses in setting the psalms in a New Testament context.

Craigie, Peter. *Psalms 1-50.* 2nd ed. WBC. Nashville: Thomas Nelson, 2004.

These volumes are uneven in quality and orthodoxy. Craigie does not accept the imprecations in the psalms as inspired: "These psalms are not the oracles of God," p. 41. See War Psalms of the Prince of Peace, below, for a good treatment of the imprecations in the psalms. These three volumes from the Word Biblical Commentary are included because of the great deal of modern research in psalm genre this century. A modern commentary is, therefore, essential. But little sermonic help will be found in these volumes.

Kidner, Derek. *Psalms 1-72.* TOTC. Downers Grove: IVP, 1981. Leicester: IVP, 1981.

Kidner, Derek. *Psalms 73-150.* TOTC. Downers Grove: IVP, 1981. Leicester: IVP, 1981.

Plummer, William S. *Psalms: A Critical and Expository Commentary with Doctrinal and Practical Remarks.* GSC. Carlisle: BoT, 1975. Edinburgh: BoT, 1975.

> *Still remains one of the best. Especially helpful are his 'doctrinal and practical remarks.'*

Tate, Marvin E. *Psalms 51-100.* WBC. Nashville: Thomas Nelson, 1990.

Consider:

Harman, Allan. *Psalms.* A Mentor Commentary. Ross-shire: CFP, 1998.

VanGemeren, Willem A. *Psalms.* EBC. Grand Rapids: Zondervan, 1991.

Wilcock, Michael. *The Message of Psalms 1-72.* BST. Downers Grove: IVP, 2001. Leicester: IVP, 2001.

Wilcock, Michael. *The Message of Psalms 73-150.* BST. Downers Grove: IVP, 2001. Leicester: IVP, 2001.

To be considered for sermon preparation:

Ainsworth, H. *Annotations on the Psalms.* Pittsburg: SDG, 1991.

> *See notes under Pentateuch.*

Boice, James M. *Psalms.* An Expositional Commentary. 3 Volumes. Grand Rapids: Baker, 2005.

Dickson, David. *Psalms.* GSC. Carlisle: BoT, 1991. Edinburgh: BT, 1991.

Spurgeon, Charles H. *A Treasury of David.* 3 Volumes. Peabody: Hendrickson, 1988.

Should definitely be considered.

Williams, Donald M. *Psalms 1-72.* TPC. Nashville: Thomas Nelson, 2002.

Williams, Donald M. *Psalms 73-150.* TPC. Nashville: Thomas Nelson, 2002.

Selected psalms:

Adams, James E. *War Psalms of the Prince of Peace: Lessons from the Imprecatory Psalms.* Phillipsburg: P & R, 1991.

See note on Craigie, above.

Beisner, E. Calvin. *Psalms of Promise: Celebrating the Majesty and Faithfulness of God.* Phillipsburg: P & R, 1994.

Psalms 1, 15, 18, 19, 22, 50, 51, 73, 74, 85, 88, 90, 101, 103, 104, 105, 107, 109, 145.

Bridges, Charles. *Psalm 119: An Exposition.* Edinburgh: BoT, 1981.

The best one volume commentary on Psalm 119.

Chantry, Walter. *Praises for the King of Kings.* Carlisle: BoT, 1991. Edinburgh: BoT, 1991.

Psalms 2, 45, 110.

Edwards, Brian. *God Cares.* Bryntirion: EPW, 1989.

Psalm 106.

Ferguson, Sinclair B. *Deserted by God?* Grand Rapids: Baker, 1996.

Psalms 13, 22, 23, 42, 43, 51, 55, 73, 102, 119:9-16, 131.

Goldingay, John. *Songs from a Strange Land: Psalms 42-51.* BST. Leicester: IVP, 1978. o/p.

Goldingay is critical but not in this book.

Klosterman, Nelson D. *Walking About Zion: Singing of Christ's Church in the Psalms.* Grand Rapids: Reformed Fellowship, 1991.

Psalms 12, 33, 44, 46, 48, 67, 79, 95, 105, 115, 122, 124, 133, 137, 147.

Lloyd Jones, D. Martyn. *Faith Tried and Triumphant.* Downers Grove: IVP, 1965. Leicester: IVP, 1965.

Psalm 73, pp. 76-217.

Lloyd Jones, D. Martyn. *Out of the Depths.* Bryntirion: EPW, 2004.

Psalm 51.

Lloyd Jones, D. Martyn. *Seeking the Face of God: Nine Reflections on the Psalms.* Wheaton: Crossway, 2005.

Psalm 14, 16, 27, 50, 63, 78, 84.

MacMillan, Douglas J. *The Lord our Shepherd.* Bridgend: Bryntirion Press, 2003.

Psalm 23.

Manton, Thomas. *Psalm 119.* 3 Volumes. Edinburgh: BoT, 1990.

Magnificent!

Owen, John. *A Practical Exposition Upon Psalm CXXX.* The Works of John Owen. Volume 6. Carlisle: BoT, 2004. Edinburgh: BoT, 2004.

This exposition of Psalm 130 is one of the finest studies on the topics of forgiveness and assurance ever penned.

Peterson, Eugene H. *A Long Obedience in the Same Direction.* Downers Grove: IVP,   2000.

Psalms of Ascent (120-134).

Robertson, O. Palmer. *Psalms for Congregational Celebration.* Darlington: EP, 1995.

Psalms 1, 2, 8, 11, 14, 15, 16, 32, 44, 80, 82, 84, 87, 91, 95, 96, 99, 106, 110, 113, 118, 126, 128, 132, 146.

Stedman, Ray C. *Psalms of Faith: A Life-Related Study from Selected Psalms.* Ventura, CA: Regall Books, 1973.

Psalms 1, 6, 19, 20, 22, 23, 34, 40, 42, 43, 45, 50, 51, 73, 84, 90, 95, 107, 109, 139.

Thomas, Derek. *Help for Hurting Christians: Reflections on Psalms.* Darlington: EP, 1991.

Psalm 5, 22, 25, 30, 54, 56, 71, 92, 119.

Thomas, Derek. *Making the Most of Your Devotional Life: Meditations on the Psalms of Ascent.* Auburn: EP, 2001. Darlington: EP, 2001.

Psalms of Ascent (120-134).

Young, Edward J. *Psalm 139: A Study in the Omniscience of God.* Edinburgh: BoT, 1965. o/p.

PROVERBS

Recommendation:

Bridges, Charles. *Proverbs.* GSC. Carlisle: BT, 1994. Edinburgh: BT, 1994.

Bridges was a first-class scholar and pastor. Though dated, his keen exegesis and searching application show that commentaries can be both scholarly and practical.

Hubbard, David A. *Proverbs.* TPC. Nashville: Thomas Nelson, 2002.

Waltke, Bruce K. *The Book of Proverbs: Chapters 1-15.* NICOT. Grand Rapids: Eerdmans, 2004.

Waltke, Bruce K. *The Book of Proverbs: Chapters 15-31.* NICOT. Grand Rapids: Eerdmans, 2005.

A lifetime achievement. This historico-grammatical commentary is sure to set the standard for commentaries on Proverbs for years to come. A definitive work.

Consider:

Atkinson, David J. *The Message of Proverbs.* BST. Downers Grove: IVP, 1997. Leicester: IVP, 1997.

Kidner, Derek. *Proverbs: An Introduction and Commentary.* TOTC. Downers Grove: IVP, 1981. Leicester: IVP, 1981.

To be considered for sermon preparation:

Arnot, William. *Laws from Heaven: Illustrations from the Book of Proverbs.* London: T. Nelson and Sons, 1857. o/p.

Very difficult to obtain, but helpful.

Brady, Gary. *Heavenly Wisdom: Proverbs Simply Explained.* Webster: EP, 2003. Darlington: EP, 2003.

Practical and devotional – much fodder for preaching Proverbs.

Lane, Eric. *Proverbs: Everyday Wisdom for Everybody.* Focus on the Bible. Ross-shire: CFP, 2000.

Turner, Charles W. *Studies in Proverbs: Wise Words in a Wicked World.* Grand Rapids: Baker, 1976. o/p.

ECCLESIASTES

Recommendation:

Bridges, Charles. *Ecclesiastes.* GCS. Carlisle: BoT, 1981. Edinburgh: BoT, 1981.

See comments above on Proverbs.

Longman III, Tremper. *The Book of Ecclesiastes.* NICOT. Grand Rapids: Eerdmans, 1998.

Takes Qohelet as 'a type of pseudonym.' Maintains two speakers: 1) Qohelet (1:12-12:7) and 2) an unnamed individual (1:1-11 and 12:8-14). Interesting but too idiosyncratic.

Consider:

Eaton, Michael. *Ecclesiastes: An Introduction and Commentary.* TOTC. Downers Grove: IVP, 1983. Leicester: IVP, 1983.

Hengstenberg, E. W. *Commentary on the Book of Ecclesiastes.* Eugene, OR: Wipf & Stock, 1998.

59

To be considered for sermon preparation:

Barnes, Peter. *Both Sides Now: Ecclesiastes and the Human Condition.* Carlisle: BoT, 2004. Edinburgh: BoT, 2004.

Ferguson, Sinclair B. *The Pundit's Folly: Chronicles of an Empty Life.* Carlisle: BoT, 1996. Edinburgh: BoT, 1996.

Kaiser, Jr., Walter C. *Ecclesiastes: Total Life.* Everyman's Bible Commentary. Chicago: Moody, 1979.

Keddie, Gordon. *The Guide to Ecclesiastes.* The Guide. Auburn: EP, 2002. Darlington: EP, 2002.

Keddie, Gordon. *Looking for the Good Life: The Search for Fulfillment in the Light of Ecclesiastes.* Phillipsburg: P & R, 1991.

Kidner, Derek. *A Time to Mourn, and a Time to Dance: Ecclesiastes and the Way of the World.* BST. Downers Grove: IVP, 1976. Leicester: IVP, 1976.

Olyott, Stuart. *A Life Worth Living and A Lord Worth Loving: Ecclesiastes and The Song of Solomon.* WCS. Welwyn: EP, 1983.

Tidball, Derek. *That's Life!: Realism and Hope for Today from Ecclesiastes.* Living Word Series. Leicester: IVP, 1989.

THE SONG OF SOLOMON

It very much depends on whether you accept the The Song of Solomon as primarily allegorical in nature. If so, then Burrowes and Durham are your choices. If not, Gledhill, Glickman, and Carr will be the choice.

Consider:

Brooks, Richard. *Song of Songs.* Focus on the Bible. Ross-shire: CFP, 1999.

Burrowes, George. *Song of Solomon.* GSC. Carlisle: BoT, 1973. London: BoT, 1973. Lafayette: Sovereign Grace, 2001.

Allegorical interpretation.

Carr, Lloyd G. *The Song of Solomon: An Introduction and Commentary.* TOTC. Downers Grove: IVP, 1984. Leicester: IVP, 1984.

A concise commentary that follows a 'natural' or 'literal' interpretation.

Durham, James. *An Exposition of the Song of Solomon.* GSC. Carlisle: BoT, 1982, Edinburgh: BoT, 1982.

A classic allegorical interpretation written by the great Scottish divine.

Ellsworth, Roger. *He is Altogether Lovely: Discovering Christ in the Song of Solomon.* Darlington: EP, 1998.

A Christological approach.

Gledhill, Tom. *The Message of Song of Songs.* BST. Downers Grove: IVP, 1994. Leicester: IVP, 1994.

Follows a non-allegorical interpretation.

Glickman, S. Craig. *Solomon's Song of Love: Let the Song of Songs Inspire Your Own Romantic Story.* West Monroe, LA: Howard Publishers, 2004.

An excellent and accessible non-allegorical commentary; includes a helpful section on interpreting the Song of Solomon.

Hess, Richard S. *Song of Songs.* Grand Rapids: Baker, 2005.

Knight, George A. *Revelation of Love: A Commentary on The Song of Songs.* ITC. Grand Rapids: Eerdmans, 1988.

A brief introduction to the Song of Songs as a 'collection of love poems.'

Longman III, Tremper. *Song of Songs.* NICOT. Grand Rapids: Eerdmans, 2001.

A more critical and exegetical study. Takes Songs as 'a collection of love poems.'

Nelson, Tommy. *The Book of Romance: What Solomon Says About Love, Sex, and Intimacy.* Nashville: Thomas Nelson, 1998.

Non-technical, non-allegorical.

Olyott, Stuart. *A Life Worth Living and A Lord Worth Loving: Ecclesiastes and The Song of Solomon.* WCS. Welwyn: EP, 1983.

A 'typical' approach.

Provan, Iain. *Ecclesiastes, Song of Songs.* NIVAC. Grand Rapids: Zondervan, 2001.

A homiletical exposition that interprets Song of Songs as a developing 'drama' of a male-female relationship.

ISAIAH

Recommendation:

Motyer, Alec J. *The Prophecy of Isaiah.* Downers Grove: IVP, 1998. Leicester: IVP, 1998.

A heavier and more detailed study than his commentary in the TOTC.

Young, Edward J. *The Book of Isaiah.* 3 Volumes in One. Grand Rapids: Eerdmans, 1992.

Young has now been replaced in the NICOT series by John N. Oswalt, a sensible commentary worth consulting, but is still preferred.

Consider:

Grogan, Geoffrey W. *Isaiah.* EBC. Grand Rapids: Zondervan, 1986.

Motyer, Alec J. *Isaiah: An Introduction and Commentary.* TOTC. Downers Grove: IVP, 1999. Leicester: IVP, 1999.

Webb, Barry. *The Message of Isaiah.* BST. Downers Grove: IVP, 1997. Leicester: IVP, 1997.

To be considered for sermon preparation:

Brent, Trent C. *Isaiah.* HOTC. Nashville: B & H, 2002.

Ellis, Charles & Norma. *The Wells of Salvation: Meditations on Isaiah.* Carlisle: BoT, 1996. Edinburgh: BoT, 1996.

Ellsworth, Roger. *The God of All Comfort.* Webster: EP, 2004. Darlington: EP, 2004.

Thomas, Derek. *God Delivers: Isaiah Simply Explained.* WCS. Auburn: MA, 2002. Darlington: EP, 2002.

JEREMIAH

Recommendation:

Thompson, J. A. *The Book of Jeremiah.* NICOT. Grand Rapids: Eerdmans, 1995.

Provides much more detailed exegetical and historical discussions than Ryken. The two compliment each other nicely.

Ryken, Philip Graham. *Jeremiah & Lamentations: From Sorrow to Hope.* PWS. Wheaton: Crossway, 2001.

A superb expositional commentary. Includes a helpful index of sermon illustrations.

Consider:

Feinberg, Charles L. *Jeremiah.* EBC. Grand Rapids: Zondervan, 1986.

Harrison, R. K. *Jeremiah and Lamentations: An Introduction and Commentary.* TOTC. Downers Grove: IVP, 1973. Leicester: IVP, 1973.

Kidner, Derek. *The Message of Jeremiah: Against Wind and Tide.* BST. Downers Grove: IVP, 1987. Leicester: IVP, 1987.

Mackay, John. L. *Jeremiah. Volume 1: Chapters 1-20.* A Mentor Commentary. Ross-shire: CFP, 2004.

Mackay, John. L. *Jeremiah. Volume 2: Chapters 21-52.* A Mentor Commentary. Ross-shire: CFP, 2004.

To be considered for sermon preparation:

Day, David. *Jeremiah: Speaking for God in a Time of Crisis.* Leicester: IVP, 1987.

McConville, J. G. *Judgment and Promise: An Interpretation of the Book of Jeremiah.* Leicester: IVP, 1993.

Peterson, Eugene H. *Run with Horses: The Quest for Life at Its Best.* Downers Grove: IVP, 1983. Leicester: IVP, 1983.

Ryken, Philip Graham. *Courage to Stand: Jeremiah's Battle Plan for Pagan Times.* Wheaton: Crossway, 1998.

Useful for small group study.

Schaeffer, Francis A. *Death in the City.* Wheaton: Crossway, 2002.

Stewart, Alexander. *Jeremiah: The Man and His Work.* Edinburgh: The Knox Press, 1971.

Dr. Stewart was a stalwart upholder of the Reformed Faith and a considerable preacher of the doctrines of grace. His Moderatorial Address to the Free Church General Assembly in 1926, A Plea for a Positive Evangel, was a model of its kind.

LAMENTATIONS

Recommendation:

House, Paul R. "Lamentations." *Song of Solomon & Lamentations.* WBC. Nashville: Thomas Nelson, 2004.

See also Ryken and Harrison above.

To be considered for sermon preparation:

Brooks, Richard. *Great is Your Faithfulness: Lamentations Simply Explained.* WCS. Darlington: EP, 1989.

EZEKIEL

Recommendation:

Block, Daniel I. *The Book of Ezekiel: Chapters 1-24.* NICOT. Grand Rapids: Eerdmans, 1997.

Block, Daniel I. *The Book of Ezekiel: Chapters 25-48.* NICOT. Grand Rapids: Eerdmans, 1998.

Technical and thorough. However, his 'Theological Implications' are proportionately brief. Though a wealth of information, a busy pastor may find Duguid a more helpful tool.

Duguid, Iain M. *Ezekiel.* NIVAC. Grand Rapids: Zondervan, 1999.

Stuart, Douglas. *Ezekiel.* TPC. Nashville: Thomas Nelson, 2002.

Exceptionally good.

Consider:

Allen, Leslie C. *Ezekiel 20-48.* WBC. Nashvile: Thomas Nelson, 1990.

Better than Brownlee on Ezekiel 1-19, which we would not consider.

Fairbairn, Patrick. *Ezekiel and the Book of his Prophecy.* Grand Rapids: Kregel, 1989.

Greenhill, William. *Ezekiel.* GSC. Carlisle: BoT, 1995. Edinburgh: BoT, 1995.

Hengstenberg, E. W. *Prophecies of The Prophet Ezekiel Elucidated.* Eugene, OR: Wipf & Stock, 2005.

Taylor, John B. *Ezekiel: An Introduction and Commentary.* TOTC. Downers Grove: IVP, 1969. Leicester: IVP, 1969.

Wright, Christopher J. H. *The Message of Ezekiel.* BST. Downers Grove: IVP, 2001. Leicester: IVP, 2001.

To be considered for sermon preparation:

Thomas, Derek. *God Strengthens: Ezekiel Simply Explained.* WCS. Darlington: EP, 1993.

DANIEL

Recommendation:

Ferguson, Sinclair B. *Daniel.* TPC. Nashville: Thomas Nelson, 2002.

Outstanding. 6th century date.

Goldingay, John E. *Daniel.* WBC. Nashville: Thomas Nelson, 1989.

Despite a 2ⁿᵈ century date and viewing the visions as pseudonymous 'quasi-prophecy,' deals ably with the text.

Longman III, Tremper. *Daniel.* NIVAC. Grand Rapids: Zondervan, 1999.

6ᵗʰ century date.

Consider:

Lucas, Ernest. *Daniel.* AOTC. Downers Grove: IVP, 2002. Leicester: IVP, 2002.

2ⁿᵈ century date but sympathetic towards an earlier date.

Young, Edward J. *Daniel.* Carlisle: BoT, 1972. Edinburgh: BoT, 1972.

To be considered for sermon preparation:

Baldwin, Joyce. *Daniel: An Introduction and Commentary.* TOTC. Downers Grove: IVP, 1981. Leicester: IVP, 1981.

Wavers a little on dating, but eventually comes down conservatively.

Boice, James Montgomery. *Daniel.* An Expositional Commentary. Grand Rapids: Baker, 2003.

Chapell, Bryan. *Standing Your Ground: Messages on Daniel.* Grand Rapids: Baker, 1989.

Fyall, Robert. *Daniel.* Focus on the Bible. Ross-shire: CFP, 1998.

Olyott, Stuart. *Dare to Stand Alone: Read and enjoy the Book of Daniel.* WCS. Welwyn: EP, 1993.

Thomas, Geoff. *Daniel: Servant of God under four kings.* Bridgend: Bryntirion Press, 1998.

Wallace, Ronald S. *The Message of Daniel.* BST. Downers Grove: IVP, 1984. Leicester: IVP, 1984.

THE MINOR PROPHETS

Recommendation:

McComiskey, Thomas Edward, ed. *The Minor Prophets: An Exegetical and Expository Commentary.* 3 Volumes. Grand Rapids: Baker, 1992-1998.

McComiskey is necessary reading for all the minor prophets.

To be considered for sermon preparation:

Boice, James Montgomery. *The Minor Prophets.* An Expositional Commentary. 2 Volumes. Grand Rapids: Baker, 2002.

Feinberg, Charles L. *The Minor Prophets.* Chicago: Moody, 1991.

Dispensational.

HOSEA

Recommendation:

Stuart, Douglas. *Hosea-Jonah.* WBC. Nashville: Thomas Nelson, 1987.

Gomer is presented typically as a harlot because she is a member of wayward Israel not because she was immoral. Clever but not convincing! Nevertheless, a very good commentary.

Consider:

Hubbard, David A. *Hosea: An Introduction and Commentary.* Downers Grove: IVP, 1990. Leicester: IVP, 1990.

Kidner, Derek. *Love to the Loveless: The Message of Hosea.* BST. Downers Grove: IVP, 1984. Leicester: IVP, 1984.

To be considered for sermon preparation:

Eaton, Michael A. *Hosea.* Focus on the Bible. Ross-shire: CFP, 1996.

Morgan, G. Campbell. *Hosea: The Heart and Holiness of God.* Grand Rapids: Baker, 1974.

JOEL

Recommendation:

Stuart, Douglas. *Hosea-Jonah.* WBC. Nashville: Thomas Nelson, 1987.

Consider:

Allen, Leslie C. *The Books of Joel, Obadiah, Jonah and Micah.* NICOT. Grand Rapids: Eerdmans, 1976.

Busenitz, Irvin. *Joel & Obadiah.* A Mentor Commentary. Ross-shire: CFP, 2003.

Hubbard, David A. *Joel & Amos: An Introduction and Commentary.* Downers Grove: IVP, 1989. Leicester: IVP, 1989.

Prior, David. *The Message of Joel, Micah& Habakkuk.* BST. Downers Grove: IVP, 1999. Leicester: IVP, 1999.

To be considered for sermon preparation:

Robertson, O. Palmer. *Prophet of the Coming Day of the Lord: The Message of Joel.* WCS. Darlington: EP, 1996.

AMOS

Recommendation:

Stuart, Douglas. *Hosea-Jonah.* WBC. Nashville: Thomas Nelson, 1987.

Consider:

Hubbard, David A. *Joel & Amos: An Introduction and Commentary.* Downers Grove: IVP, 1989. Leicester: IVP, 1989.

Motyer, J. Alec. *The Day of the Lion.* BST. Downers Grove: IVP, 1974. Leicester: IVP, 1974.

Smith, Gary V. *Amos.* A Mentor Commentary. Ross-shire: CFP, 2001.

To be considered for sermon preparation:

Keddie, Gordon J. *The Lord is his Name: Studies in Amos.* WCS. Welwyn: EP, 1986.

OBADIAH

Recommendation:

Stuart, Douglas. *Hosea-Jonah.* WBC. Nashville: Thomas Nelson, 1987.

Consider:

Allen, Leslie C. *The Books of Joel, Obadiah, Jonah and Micah.* NICOT. Grand Rapids: Eerdmans, 1976.

Baker, W. David. "Obadiah." *Obadiah, Jonah and Micah: An Introduction and Commentary.* TOTC. Downers Grove: IVP, 1988. Leicester: IVP, 1988.

Busenitz, Irvin. *Joel & Obadiah.* A Mentor Commentary. Ross-shire: CFP, 2003.

Marbury, Edward. *Obadiah and Habakkuk.* Minneapolis: KK, 1979.

JONAH

Recommendation:

Stuart, Douglas. *Hosea-Jonah.* WBC. Nashville: Thomas Nelson, 1987.

Consider:

Alexander, T. Desmond. "Jonah." *Obadiah, Jonah and Micah: An Introduction and Commentary.* TOTC. Downers Grove: IVP, 1988. Leicester: IVP, 1988.

Allen, Leslie C. *The Books of Joel, Obadiah, Jonah and Micah.* NICOT. Grand Rapids: Eerdmans, 1976.

To be considered for sermon preparation:

Fairbairn, Patrick. *Jonah: His Life, Character, and Mission.* Eugene, OR: Wipf & Stock, 2004.

Ferguson, Sinclair B. *Man Overboard!: The Story of Jonah.* Glasgow: Pickering and Inglis, 1981.

Keddie, Gordon J. *Preacher on the Run: The Message of Jonah.* WCS. Welwyn: EP, 1986.

Legg, John. *When We Don't Understand: God's Ways with Jonah and Habakkuk.* WCS. Darlington: EP, 1993.

Mackay, John L. *God's Just Demands: Jonah, Micah, Nahum, Habakkuk & Zephaniah.* Focus on the Bible. Ross-shire: CFP, 1999.

Martin, Hugh. *The Prophet Jonah.* Carlisle: BoT, 2001. Edinburgh: BoT, 2001.

Peterson, Eugene H. *Under the Unpredictable Plan: An Exploration in Vocational Holiness.* Grand Rapids: Eerdmans, 1994.

Robertson, O. Palmer. *Jonah.* Carlisle: BoT, 1990. Edinburgh: BoT, 1990.

MICAH

Recommendation:

Allen, Leslie C. *The Books of Joel, Obadiah, Jonah and Micah.* NICOT. Grand Rapids: Eerdmans, 1994.

Waltke, Bruce K. "Micah." *Obadiah, Jonah and Micah: An Introduction and Commentary.* TOTC. Downers Grove: IVP, 1988. Leicester: IVP, 1988.

Consider:

Prior, David. *The Message of Joel, Micah & Habakkuk.* BST. Downers Grove: IVP, 1999. Leicester: IVP, 1999.

To be considered for sermon preparation:

Bentley, Michael. *Balancing the Books: Micah and Nahum Simply Explained.* WCS. Darlington: EP, 1994.

Calvin, John. *Sermons on the Book of Micah.* Phillipsburg: P & R, 2003.

Grant, George. *The Micah Mandate.* Chicago: Moody, 1997.

Micah 6:8.

Mackay, John L. *God's Just Demands: Jonah, Micah, Nahum, Habakkuk & Zephaniah.* Focus on the Bible. Ross-shire: CFP, 1999.

NAHUM

Recommendation:

Robertson, O. Palmer. *Nahum, Habakkuk and Zephaniah.* NICOT. Grand Rapids: Eerdmans, 1994.

> *A masterfully done commentary. Nicely weds a redemptive-historical hermeneutic with a pastor's touch.*

Consider:

Baker, David. *Nahum, Habakkuk, Zephaniah: An Introduction and Commentary.* TOTC. Downers Grove: IVP, 1989. Leicester: IVP, 1989.

Patterson, Richard D. *Nahum, Habakkuk, Zephaniah.* WEC. Chicago: Moody, 1991.

To be considered for sermon preparation:

Bentley, Michael. *Balancing the Books: Micah and Nahum Simply Explained.* WCS. Darlington: EP, 1994.

Mackay, John L. *God's Just Demands: Jonah, Micah, Nahum, Habakkuk & Zephaniah.* Focus on the Bible. Ross-shire: CFP, 1999.

HABAKKUK

Recommendation:

Robertson, O. Palmer. *Nahum, Habakkuk and Zephaniah.* NICOT. Grand Rapids: Eerdmans, 1994.

See above on Nahum.

Consider:

Baker, David. *Nahum, Habakkuk, Zephaniah: An Introduction and Commentary.* TOTC. Downers Grove: IVP, 1989. Leicester: IVP, 1989.

Patterson, Richard D. *Nahum, Habakkuk, Zephaniah.* WEC. Chicago: Moody, 1991.

Marbury, Edward. *Obadiah and Habakkuk.* Minneapolis: KK, 1979.

Prior, David. *The Message of Joel, Micah& Habakkuk.* BST. Downers Grove: IVP, 1999. Leicester: IVP, 1999.

To be considered for sermon preparation:

Legg, John. *When We Don't Understand: God's Ways with Jonah and Habakkuk.* WCS. Darlington: EP, 1992.

Lloyd-Jones, D. Martyn. *Faith Tried and Triumphant.* Grand Rapids: Baker, 1993.

Mackay, John L. *God's Just Demands: Jonah, Micah, Nahum, Habakkuk & Zephaniah.* Focus on the Bible. Ross-shire: CFP, 1999.

ZEPHANIAH

Recommendation:

Robertson, O. Palmer. *Nahum, Habakkuk and Zephaniah.* NICOT. Grand Rapids: Eerdmans, 1994.

See above on Nahum.

Consider:

Baker, David. *Nahum, Habakkuk, Zephaniah: An Introduction and Commentary.* TOTC. Downers Grove: IVP, 1988. Leicester: IVP, 1988.

Patterson, Richard D. *Nahum, Habakkuk, Zephaniah.* WEC. Chicago: Moody, 1991.

To be considered for sermon preparation:

Mackay, John L. *God's Just Demands: Jonah, Micah, Nahum, Habakkuk & Zephaniah.* Focus on the Bible. Ross-shire: CFP, 1999.

Webber, Daniel. *The Coming of the Warrior-King: Zephaniah Simply Explained.* WCS. Webster: EP, 2004. Darlington: EP, 2004.

HAGGAI

Recommendation:

Verhoef, Peter A. *Haggai and Malachi.* NICOT. Grand Rapids: Eerdmans, 1994.

Consider:

Baldwin, Joyce. *Haggai, Zechariah, Malachi: An Introduction and Commentary.* TOTC. Downers Grove: IVP, 1972. Leicester: IVP, 1972.

Moore, T. V. *Haggai, Zechariah and Malachi.* GSC. Carlisle: BoT, 1979. Edinburgh: BoT, 1979.

To be considered for sermon preparation:

Bentley, Michael. *Building God's Glory: Haggai and Zechariah.* Welwyn: EP, 1993.

Mackay, John L. *Haggai, Zechariah & Malachi: God's Restored People.* Focus on the Bible. Ross-shire: CFP, 1994.

ZECHARIAH

Recommendation:

No recommendation on a single volume; see above on The Minor Prophets Collective.

Consider:

Baldwin, Joyce. *Haggai, Zechariah, Malachi: An Introduction and Commentary.* TOTC. Downers Grove: IVP, 1972. Leicester: IVP, 1972.

Baron, David. *Zechariah: A Commentary on His Visions & Prophecies.* Grand Rapids: Kregel, 2002.

Kline, Meredith G. *Glory in Our Midst: A Biblical-Theological Reading of Zechariah's Night Visions.* Overland Park, KS: Two Age Press, 2001.

Leupold, H. C. *Exposition of Zechariah.* Grand Rapids: Baker, 1965.

Moore, T. V. *Haggai, Zechariah and Malachi.* GSC. Carlisle: BoT, 1979. Edinburgh: BoT, 1979.

To be considered for sermon preparation:

Bentley, Michael. *Building God's Glory: Haggai and Zechariah.* Welwyn: EP, 1993.

Mackay, John L. *Haggai, Zechariah & Malachi: God's Restored People.* Focus on the Bible. Ross-shire: CFP, 1994.

MALACHI
Recommendation:

Kaiser, Jr., Walter. *Malachi: God's Unchanging Love.* Grand Rapids: Baker, 1984.

Consider:

Baldwin, Joyce. *Haggai, Zechariah, Malachi: An Introduction and Commentary.* TOTC. Downers Grove: IVP, 1972. Leicester: IVP, 1972.

Moore, T. V. *Haggai, Zechariah and Malachi.* GSC. Carlisle: BoT, 1979. Edinburgh: BoT, 1979.

Verhoef, Peter A. *Haggai and Malachi.* NICOT. Grand Rapids: Eerdmans, 1987.

To consider for sermon preparation:

Benton, John. *Losing Touch with the Living God: The Message of Malachi.* WCS. Welwyn: EP, 1985.

Mackay, John L. *God's Restored People: Haggai, Zechariah & Malachi.* Focus on the Bible. Ross-shire: CFP, 1994.

Morgan, G. Campbell. *Malachi's Message for Today.* Eugene, OR: Wipf & Stock, 1998.

ESSENTIAL COMMENTARIES ON THE NEW TESTAMENT

COMPLETE COMMENTARY ON THE NEW TESTAMENT

Recommendation:

Hendriksen, William and Simon Kistemaker. *New Testament Commentary.* 12 Volumes. Grand Rapids: Baker, 2002.

> *Though some volumes are better than others, this is the best complete set of New Testament commentaries. From an evangelical, reformed perspective. Should be consulted on each book.*

Consider:

Trapp, John. *Trapp's Commentary on the New Testament.* Grand Rapids: Baker, 1982.

MATTHEW

Recommendation:

Carson, D. A. *Matthew.* EBC. Grand Rapids: Zondervan, 1984.

Morris, Leon. *The Gospel According to Matthew.* PNTC. Grand
Rapids: Eerdmans, 1992. Leicester: IVP, 1992.

Both Carson and Morris are sure and trusty guides.

Consider:

Blomberg, Craig L. *Matthew.* NAC. Nashville: B & H, 1992.

Dickson, David. *Matthew.* GSC. Carlisle: BoT, 1981. Edinburgh: BoT,
1981.

France, R. T. *Matthew: An Introduction and Commentary.* TNTC.
Grand Rapids: Eerdmans, 1985. Leicester: IVP, 1985.

*France adopts a view that Matthew 24:1-35 refers entirely to
the destruction of Jerusalem, which Postmillennialists have
also done, e.g. J. Marcellus Kirk, Eschatology of Victory
(Phillipsburg: P & R, 1971). A better analysis and exposition
of these eschatological chapters is that of John Murray, "The
Interadventual Period and the Advent: Matthew 24 and 25,"
in the Collected Writing of John Murray, vol. 2 (Edinburgh:
BoT, 1977), pp. 387-400.*

Gundry, Robert H. *Matthew: A Commentary on His Handbook for a
Mixed Church under Persecution.* 2nd ed. Grand Rapids: Eerdmans,
1994.

*Mention is made of Gundry's work because of its serious
scholarship. However, his emphasis on redaction criticism
will frustrate the busy pastor.*

Keener, Craig S. *A Commentary on the Gospel of Matthew.* Grand
Rapids: Eerdmans, 1999.

*Similar to Gundry, Keener writes a socio-historical
commentary and represents the best of current scholarship*

on Matthew but is little help to preachers. Does not believe Matthew wrote the gospel. See also his smaller work in the IVP New Testament Commentary Series, Matthew (Downers Grove: IVP, 1997).

Mounce, Robert H. *Matthew.* NIBC. Peabody: Hendrickson, 1991.

To be considered for sermon preparation:

Boice, James Montgomery. *Matthew.* An Expositional Commentary. 2 Volumes. Grand Rapids: Baker, 2001.

Legg, John. *The King and His Kingdom: Matthew Simply Explained.* WCS. Webster: EP, 2004. Darlington: EP, 2004.

Lloyd-Jones, D. Martyn. *The Heart of the Gospel: Who Jesus Is and Why He Came.* Wheaton: Crossway, 1991.

Sermons on Matthew 11.

Jackman, David. *Taking Jesus Seriously: The Teaching of Jesus in Matthew.* Ross-shire: CFP, 1994.

MacArthur, John. *Matthew.* The MacArthur New Testament Commentary. 4 Volumes. Chicago: Moody, 1985.

Helpful for outlining a text and for application. Dispensational on Matt. 24-25.

Price, Charles. *Matthew.* Focus on the Bible. Ross-shire: CFP, 1998.

Ryle, J. C. "Matthew." *Expository Thoughts on the Gospels.* Carlisle: BoT, 1986. Edinburgh: BoT, 1986.

Sermon on the Mount:

Boice, James Montgomery *The Sermon on the Mount.* An Expositional Commentary. Grand Rapids: Baker, 2002.

Carson, D. A. *The Sermon on the Mount: An Evangelical Exposition of Matthew 5-7.* Grand Rapids: Baker, 1986.

Ferguson, Sinclair B. *The Sermon on the Mount.* Carlisle: BoT, 1988. Edinburgh: BoT, 1988.

Hughes, R. Kent. *Sermon on the Mount.* PWS. Wheaton: Crossway, 2001.

Lloyd-Jones, D. Martyn. *Studies in the Sermon on the Mount.* 2 Volumes. Grand Rapids: Eerdmans, 1960.

Stott, John. *The Message of the Sermon on the Mount.* BST. Downers Grove: IVP, 1993. Leicester: IVP, 1993.

Beatitudes:

Blanchard, John. *The Beatitudes for today.* Kent: Day One Publications, 1996.

Burroughs, Jeremiah. *Burroughs on the Beatitudes.* Beaver Falls, PA: Soli Deo Gloria, 1992.

Duguid, Iain M. *Hero of Heroes: Seeing Christ in the Beatitudes.* Phillipsburg: P & R, 2001.

Johnson, Terry L. *When Grace Transforms: The Character of Christ's Disciples Put Forward in the Beatitudes.* Ross-shire: CFP, 2002.

Watson, Thomas. *The Beatitudes.* Carlisle: BoT, 1985. Edinburgh: BoT, 1985.

The Lord's Prayer:

Johnson, Terry L. *When Grace Comes Alive: Living through the Lord's Prayer.* Ross-shire: CFP, 2004.

Ryken, Philip Graham. *When You Pray: Making the Lord's Prayer Your Own.* Wheaton, IL: Crossway, 2000

Thomas, Derek. *Praying the Saviour's Way: Let Jesus' prayer reshape your prayer life.* Ross-shire: CFP, 2002.

Watson, Thomas. *The Lord's Prayer.* Carlisle: BoT, 1994. Edinburgh: BoT, 1994.

Witsius, Herman. *Sacred Dissertations on The Lord's Prayer.* Phillipsburg: P & R, 1994.

MARK

Recommendation:

Cranfield, C. E. B. *The Gospel According to St. Mark.* The Cambridge Greek Testament Commentary. Cambridge: CUP, 1959.

Lane, William. *Mark.* NICNT. Grand Rapids: Eerdmans, 1974.

Consider:

Cole, R. Alan. *Mark: An Introduction and Commentary.* TNTC. Grand Rapids: Eerdmans, 1989. Leicester: IVP, 1990.

Edwards, James. *Mark.* PNTC. Grand Rapids: Eerdmans, 2001.

France, R. T. *Mark.* NIGTC. Grand Rapids: Eerdmans, 2002.

Garland, David E. *Mark.* NIVAC. Grand Rapids: Zondervan, 1996.

Gundry, Robert. *Mark: A Commentary on His Apology for the Cross.* Grand Rapids: Eerdmans, 2000.

This book is very expensive, but contains a mine of useful information that you will find nowhere else.

To be considered for sermon preparation:

Ferguson, Sinclair B. *Let's Study Mark.* Carlisle: BoT, 1999. Edinburgh: BoT, 1999.

Grogan, Geoffrey. *Mark: Good News from Jerusalem.* Focus on the Bible. Ross-shire: CFP, 2003.

Hughes, R. Kent. *Mark 1:1-9:1.* PWS. Wheaton: Crossway, 1989.

Hughes, R. Kent. *Mark 9:2-16:20.* PWS. Wheaton: Crossway, 1989.

English, David. *The Message of Mark.* BST. Downers Grove: IVP, 1992. Leicester: IVP, 1992.

Philip, George M. *Daily Grace from the Gospel of Mark.* Auburn: EP, 2001. Darlington: EP, 2001.

Ryle, J. C. "Mark." *Expository Thoughts on the Gospels.* Carlisle: BoT, 1998. Edinburgh: BoT, 1998.

Uprichard, Harry. *A Son is Revealed: Discovering Christ in the Gospel of Mark.* Darlington: EP, 1999.

LUKE

Recommendation:

Block, Darrell L. *Luke: 1:1-9:50.* BECNT. Grand Rapids: Baker, 1994.

Block, Darrell L. *Luke: 9:51-24:53.* BECNT. Grand Rapids: Baker, 1996.

Block is a preeminent scholar on Luke. These two gigantic commentaries are to be preferred to Marshall. There is a great deal of theological comment in these volumes which make them very useful for sermon preparation. However, Bock does not always come down on one side in issues of controversy. He is a progressive dispensationalist.

Block, Darrell L. *Luke.* IVPNT. Downers Grove: IVP, 1994. Leicester: IVP, 1994.

A smaller version of the commentary above.

Block, Darrell L. *Luke.* NIVAC. Grand Rapids: Zondervan, 1996.

Yes, a third commentary on Luke! This will be the most helpful for application.

Consider:

Geldenhuys, Norval. *The Gospel of Luke.* NICNT. Grand Rapids: Eerdmans, 1996.

Has been replaced by Joel B. Green.

Marshall, I. Howard. *Commentary on Luke.* NIGTC. Grand Rapids: Eerdmans, 1978.

Problematic.

Morris, Leon. *Luke: An Introduction and Commentary.* TNTC. Grand Rapids: Eerdmans, 1994. Leicester: IVP, 1988.

Stein, Robert H. *Luke.* NAC. Nashville: B & H, 1992.

Clear, concise comments on each phrase.

To be considered for sermon preparation:

Blanchard, John. *Luke Comes Alive.* Welwyn: EP, 2005.

Gooding, David. *According to Luke: A New Exposition of the Third Gospel.* Grand Rapids: Eerdmans, 1987. Leicester: IVP, 1987.

Hughes, R. Kent. *Luke 1:1-11:28.* PWS. Wheaton: Crossway, 1998.

Hughes, R. Kent. *Luke 11:29-24:53.* PWS. Wheaton: Crossway, 1998.

Maclaren, Alexander. *St. Luke.* Expositions of Holy Scripture. Whitefish, MT: Kessinger Publishing, 2004.

Milne, Douglas, *Let's Study Luke.* Carlisle: BoT, 2005. Edinburgh: BoT, 2005.

Ryle, J. C. "Luke." *Expository Thoughts on the Gospels.* 2 Volumes. Carlisle: BoT, 1997-1998. Edinburgh: BoT, 1997-1998.

Sproul, R. C. *A Walk with Jesus: Enjoying the Company of Christ.* Ross-shire: CFP, 1999.

Wilcock, Michael. *The Message of Luke.* BST. Downers Grove: IVP, 1997. Leicester: IVP, 1997.

JOHN

Recommendation:

Carson, D. A. *The Gospel According to John.* PNTC. Grand Rapids: Eerdmans, 1991.

The best!

Ridderbos, Herman. *The Gospel of John: A Theological Commentary.* Grand Rapids: Eerdmans, 1997.

A masterful redemptive-historical commentary.

Consider:

Barrett, C. K. *The Gospel According to St. John.* London: SPCK, 1955.

Barrett is undoubtedly the best commentary on John as far as the Greek text is concerned, though it should be read with discernment. Barrett is not an evangelical! He sits loose from John's historical references.

Beasley-Murray, George R. *John.* WBC. Nashville: Thomas Nelson, 1999.

Read with care.

Brown, Raymond. *The Gospel According to John.* 2 Volumes. ABS. New York: Doubleday, 1966, 1970.

Bear in mind that Brown is Roman Catholic. Beware of the ever-present Eucharistic interpretations, and ignore the literary critical analysis.

Hutcheson, George. *John.* GSC. Carlisle: BT, 1972. Edinburgh: BT, 1972.

Keddie, Gordon J. *A Study Commentary on John. Volume 1: Chapters 1-12.* Auburn: EP, 2001. Darlington: EP, 2001.

Keddie, Gordon J. *A Study Commentary on John. Volume 2: Chapters 13-21.* Auburn: EP, 2001. Darlington: EP, 2001.

Köstenberger, Andreas J. *John.* BECNT. Grand Rapids: Baker, 2004.

Kruse, Colin G. *John: An Introduction and Commentary.* Grand Rapids: Eerdmans, 2004. Leicester: IVP, 2003.

Morris, Leon. *The Gospel According to John.* NICNT. Grand Rapids: Eerdmans, 1994.

To be considered for sermon preparation:

Boice, James Montgomery. *The Gospel According to John.* An Expositional Commentary. 5 Volumes. Grand Rapids: Baker, 1999.

Bruce, F. F. *The Gospel & Epistles of John.* 2 Volumes in one. Grand Rapids: Eerdmans, 1983.

Carson, D. A. *Jesus and His Friends: His Farewell Message and Prayer in John 14-17.* Living Word Series. Grand Rapids: Baker, 1986. Leicester: IVP, 1986.

Hughes, R. Kent. *John.* PWS. Wheaton: Crossway, 1999.

Johnston, Mark. *Let's Study John.* Carlisle: BoT, 2003. Edinburgh: BoT, 2003.

Köstenberger, Andreas J. *Encountering John.* EBS. Grand Rapids: Baker, 2004.

Lloyd-Jones, D. Martyn. *The Path to Truth Happiness: John 2.* Grand Rapids: Baker, 1999.

Lloyd-Jones, D. Martyn. *The Quiet Heart.* Wheaton: Crossway, 1995.

John 14.

Lloyd-Jones, D. Martyn. *The Assurance of our Salvation: Studies in John 17.* Wheaton: Crossway, 2000.

Previously four volumes.

Milne, Bruce. *The Message of John.* BST. Downers Grove: IVP, 1993. Leicester: IVP, 1993.

Morgan, G. Campbell. *The Gospel According to John.* Eugene, OR: Wipf & Stock, 2004.

Morris, Leon. *Expository Reflections on the Gospel of John.* 4 Volumes in one. Grand Rapids: Baker, 1990.

Newton, George. *John 17.* Carlisle: BoT, 1995.

Ross, Charles. *The Inner Sanctuary: An Exposition of John Chapters 13-17.* Carlisle: BoT, 1996. Edinburgh: BoT, 1996.

Ryan, Joseph "Skip." *That You May Believe: New Life in the Son.* Studies in the Gospel of John. Wheaton: Crossway, 2003.

Ryle, J. C. "John." *Expository Thoughts on the Gospels.* 3 Volumes. Carlisle: BoT, 1997-1999. Edinburgh: BoT, 1997-1999.

ACTS

Recommendation:

F. F. Bruce, *The Book of Acts.* NICNT. Grand Rapids: Eerdmans, 1988.

A classic. Strong on history and more accessible than his Greek commentary below.

Consider:

Alexander, J. A. *The Acts of the Apostles.* GSC. Carlisle: BoT, 1963. Edinburgh: BoT, 1963.

Bruce, F. F. *The Acts of the Apostles: Greek Text with Introduction and Commentary.* Grand Rapids: Eerdmans, 1990. Leicester: IVP, 1990.

Great on Greek; terrible on theology.

Larkin, Jr., William J. *Acts.* IVPNT. Downers Grove: IVP, 1995. Leicester: IVP, 1995.

Longenecker, Richard N. *Acts.* EBC. Grand Rapids: Zondervan, 1996.

Marshall, I. H. *Acts: An Introduction and Commentary.* TNTC. Grand Rapids: Eerdmans, 1992. Leicester: IVP, 1988.

To be considered for sermon preparation:

Boice, James Montgomery. *Acts.* An Expositional Commentary. Grand Rapids: Baker, 1997.

Fernando, Ajith. *Acts.* NIVAC. Grand Rapids: Zondervan, 1998.

Hughes, R. Kent. *Acts.* PWS. Wheaton: Crossway, 1996.

Johnson, Dennis E. *The Message of Acts in the History of Redemption.* Phillipsburg: P & R, 1997.

Johnson, Dennis E. *Let's Study Acts.* Carlisle: BoT, 2003. Edinburgh: BoT, 2003.

Morgan, G. Campbell. *The Acts of the Apostles.* Grand Rapids: Revell, 1979.

Stott, John R. W. *The Message of Acts.* BST. Downers Grove: IVP, 1994. Leicester: IVP, 1994.

Four volume exposition on Acts by D. Martyn Lloyd Jones:

Lloyd-Jones, D. Martyn. *Studies in the Book of Acts: Authentic Christianity.* Volume 1. Wheaton: Crossway, 2000.

Acts 1-3.

Lloyd-Jones, D. Martyn. *Studies in the Book of Acts: Courageous Christianity.* Volume 2. Wheaton: Crossway, 2001.

Acts 4-5.

Lloyd-Jones, D. Martyn. *Studies in the Book of Acts: Victorious Christianity.* Volume 3. Wheaton: Crossway, 2003.

Acts 5-6.

Lloyd-Jones, D. Martyn. *Studies in the Book of Acts: Glorious Christianity.* Volume 4. Crossway: Wheaton: 2004.

Acts 7.

ROMANS

Recommendation:

Cranfield, C. E. B. *Romans*. NICC. 2 Volumes. Edinburgh: T & T Clark: 2004.

Moo, Douglas J. *The Epistle to the Romans*. NICNT. Grand Rapids: Eerdmans, 1996.

A colossal commentary (over a thousand pages!). Moo's interpretation of Romans 7 is definitely not to be recommended; nevertheless, his commentary has already become a standard and has more to offer than Cranfield. See his contribution on Romans in the New Bible Commentary, 21st Century Edition for a shorter treatment.

Moo, Douglas J. *Encountering the Book of Romans*. EBS. Grand Rapids: Baker, 2002.

Moo, Douglas J. *Romans*. NIVAC. Grand Rapids: Zondervan, 2000.

Murray, John. *The Epistle to the Romans*. NICNT. 2 Volumes in one. Grand Rapids: Eerdmans, 1997.

Though replaced by Moo, this ranks as one of the finest Reformed commentaries ever written. Murray was a master exegete and brilliant systematician. Every shelf should have a copy of this commentary.

Schreiner, Thomas. *Romans*. BECNT. Grand Rapids: Baker, 1998.

Coupled with Murray on the one hand and Moo on the other, you will gain a firm exegetical and theological grasp of a text. Note that since his commentary, Schreiner has changed his view from seeing righteousness as 'transformative' to 'forensic,' see Paul: Apostle of God's Glory in Christ (Downers Grove: IVP, 2001), p. 192.n2.

Consider:

Haldane, Robert. *Romans.* GSC. Carlisle: BT, 1989. Edinburgh: BT, 1989.

Hodge, Charles. *Romans.* GSC. Carlisle: BT, 1972. Edinburgh: BT, 1972.

Hodge is a classic Reformed commentary on Romans, though the best of what he says is in Murray.

Morris, Leon. *The Epistle to the Romans.* PNTC. Grand Rapids: Eerdmans, 1988.

Mounce, Robert H. *Romans.* NAC. Nashville: B & H, 1995.

Plumer, William S. *Commentary on Romans.* Grand Rapids: Kregel, 1993.

To be considered for sermon preparation:

Barnett, Paul. *Romans: The Revelation of God's Righteousness.* Focus on the Bible. Ross-shire: CFP, 2003.

Boice, James Montgomery. *Romans.* An Expositional Commentary. 4 Volumes. Grand Rapids: Baker, 1991-1995.

Carson, D. A. *A Call to Spiritual Reformation: Priorities from Paul and his Prayers.* Grand Rapids: Baker, 1992. Leicester: IVP, 1992.

Chapter 12, "Prayer for Ministry," on Romans 15:14-33.

Clark, A. Benjamin R. *Delight for a Wretched Man: Romans 7 and the doctrine of sanctification.* WCS. Darlington: EP, 1993.

Fraser, James (of Alness). *A Treatise on Sanctification: An Explication of Romans Chapters 6, 7, & 8:1-4.* Audubon, NJ: Old Paths Publications, 1992.

Hughes, R. Kent. *Romans.* PWS. Wheaton: Crossway, 1991.

Jacomb, Thomas. *Romans 8: Versus One to Four.* Carlisle: BoT, 1996. Edinburgh: BoT, 1996.

MacArthur, John. *Romans.* The MacArthur New Testament Commentary. 2 Volumes. Chicago: Moody, 1994-1995.

Dispensational regarding Romans 11.

Murray, John. *The Imputation of Adam's Sin.* Phillipsburg: P & R, 1993.

Olyott, Stuart. *The Gospel as it Really is: Paul's Epistle to the Romans simply explained.* WCS. Welwyn: EP, 1979.

Ortlund, Jr., Raymond C. *A Passion for God: Prayers and Meditation on the Book of Romans.* Wheaton: Crossway, 2002.

Piper, John. *The Justification of God: An Exegetical and Theological Study of Romans 9:1-23.* 2nd ed. Grand Rapids: Baker, 1993.

Sproul, R. C. *The Gospel of God: An Exposition of Romans.* Ross-shire: CFP, 1999.

Stott, John R. W. *The Message of Romans.* Downers Grove: IVP, 2001. Leicester: IVP, 2001.

Fourteen volume exposition on Romans by D. Martyn Lloyd Jones:

Lloyd-Jones, D. Martyn. *Romans 1: The Gospel of God.* Edinburgh: BoT, 1998.

Lloyd-Jones, D. Martyn. *Romans 2:1-3:20: The Righteous Judgment of God.* Edinburgh: BoT, 1998.

Lloyd-Jones, D. Martyn. *Romans 3:20-4:25: Atonement and Justification.* Edinburgh: BoT, 1971.

Lloyd-Jones, D. Martyn. *Romans 5: Assurance.* Edinburgh: BoT, 1972.

Lloyd-Jones, D. Martyn. *Romans 6: The New Man.* Edinburgh: BT, 1998.

Lloyd-Jones, D. Martyn. *Romans 7:1-8:4: The Law: Its Functions and Limits.* Edinburgh: BoT, 1974.

Lloyd-Jones, D. Martyn. *Romans 8:5-17: The Sons of God.* Edinburgh: BoT, 1975.

Lloyd-Jones, D. Martyn. *Romans 8:17-39: The Final Perseverance of the Saints.* Edinburgh: BoT, 1998.

Lloyd-Jones, D. Martyn. *Romans 9: God's Sovereign Purpose.* Edinburgh: BoT, 1992.

Lloyd-Jones, D. Martyn. *Romans 10: Saving Faith.* Edinburgh: BT, 1998.

Lloyd-Jones, D. Martyn. *Romans 11: To God's Glory.* Edinburgh: BT, 1999.

Lloyd-Jones, D. Martyn. *Romans 12: Christian Conduct.* Edinburgh: BoT, 2000.

Lloyd-Jones, D. Martyn. *Romans 13: Life in Two Kingdoms.* Edinburgh: BoT, 2003.

Lloyd-Jones, D. Martyn. *Romans 14:1-17: Liberty and Conscience.* Edinburgh: BT, 2004.

Unparalleled example of expository preaching, though few will follow his exposition of Romans 7:14ff.

1 CORINTHIANS

Recommendation:

Hodge, Charles. *I & II Corinthians.* GSC. Carlisle: BoT, 1998. Edinburgh: BoT, 1998.

Truly a classic.

Naylor, Peter. *A Study Commentary on 1 Corinthians.* EPSC. Webster: EP, 2004. Darlington: EP, 2004.

Pratt, Richard. *1 and 2 Corinthians.* HNTC. Nashville: B & H, 2000.

A nice blend of exposition, theology, and application.

Consider:

Barrett, C. K. *First Epistle to the Corinthians.* Blacks New Testament Commentary. Peabody: Hendrickson, 1993.

Blomberg, Craig. *1 Corinthians.* NIVAC. Grand Rapids: Zondervan, 1995.

Good work. Tends towards an egalitarian view of women and a non-cessationist view of gifts.

Bruce, F. F. *I & II Corinthians.* NCB. Grand Rapids: Eerdmans, 1980.

Fee, Gordon F. *The First Epistle to the Corinthians.* NICNT. Grand Rapids: Eerdmans, 1987.

Care! Fee has a few problems, e.g. he regards 1 Cor. 14:33b-35 as an interpolation!

Garland, David E. *1 Corinthians.* BECNT. Grand Rapids: Baker, 2003.

98

Grosheide, F. W. *The First Epistle to the Corinthians.* NICNT. Grand Rapids: Eerdmans, 1976.

> *Replaced by Fee in the NICNT series.*

Morris, Leon. *1 Corinthians: An Introduction and Commentary.* TNTC. Grand Rapids: Eerdmans, 1986. Leicester: IVP, 1985.

Thiselton, Anthony C. *The First Epistle to the Corinthians.* NIGTC. Grand Rapids: Eerdmans, 2000.

> *Comprehensive and critical. Pays close attention to socio-historical development.*

To be considered for sermon preparation:

Barnett, Paul. *1 Corinthians: Holiness and Hope of a Rescued People.* Focus on the Bible. Ross-shire: CFP, 2000.

Carson, D. A. *Showing the Spirit: A Theological Exposition of 1 Corinthians 12-14.* Grand Rapids: Baker, 1996.

Jackman, David. *Let's Study 1 Corinthians.* Carlisle: BoT, 2004. Edinburgh: BoT, 2004.

Prior, David. *The Message of 1 Corinthians.* BST. Downers Grove: IVP, 1988. Leicester: IVP, 1988.

2 CORINTHIANS

Recommendation:

Hodge, Charles. *I & II Corinthians.* GSC. Carlisle: BoT, 1998. Edinburgh: BoT, 1998.

Hughes, P. E. *The Second Epistle to the Corinthians.* NICNT. Grand Rapids: Eerdmans, 1962.

Has been replaced by Paul Barnett in the NICNT series.

Naylor, Peter. *A Study Commentary on 2 Corinthians. Volume 1: Chapter 1-7.* Auburn: EP, 2002. Darlington: EP, 2002.

Naylor, Peter. *A Study Commentary on 2 Corinthians. Volume 2: Chapters 8-13.* Auburn: EP, 2002. Darlington: EP, 2002.

Pratt, Richard. *1 and 2 Corinthians.* HNTC. Nashville: B & H, 2000.

See comments on 1 Corinthians above.

Consider:

Barrett, C. K. *Second Epistle to the Corinthians.* BNTC. Peabody: Hendrickson, 1993.

Bruce, F. F. *I & II Corinthians.* NCB. Grand Rapids: Eerdmans, 1996.

Kruse, Colin. *2 Corinthians: An Introduction and Commentary.* TNTC. Grand Rapids: Eerdmans, 1987. Leicester: IVP, 1987.

See also his entry in the New Bible Commentary, 21ˢᵗ Century Edition.

Martin, Ralph P. *2 Corinthians.* WBC. Waco: Word, 1986.

This is infuriatingly speculative and muddled in parts for what purports to be an evangelical commentary. However, there is little on 2 Corinthians and you may be forced to consider it.

To be considered for sermon preparation:

Arthur, J. Philip. *Strength in Weakness: 2 Corinthians Simply Explained.* WCS. Webster: EP, 2004. Darlington: EP, 2004.

Barnett, Paul. *The Message of 2 Corinthians.* BST. Downers Grove: IVP, 1988. Leicester: IVP, 1988.

See also his exegetical commentary, The Second Epistle to the Corinthians, NICNT (Grand Rapids: Eerdmans, 1997).

Carson, D. A. *From Triumphalism to Maturity: A new exposition of 2 Corinthians 10-13.* Downers Grove: IVP, 1986. Leicester: IVP, 1986.

Grogan, Geoffrey. *2 Corinthians.* Focus on the Bible. Ross-shire: CFP, 1997.

Kelly, Douglas F. *New Life in the Wasteland: 2 Corinthians on the Cost and Glory of Christian Ministry.* Ross-shire: CFP, 2003.

Prime, Derek. *Let's Study 2 Corinthians.* Carlisle: BoT, 2000. Edinburgh: BoT, 2000.

GALATIANS

Recommendation:

Bruce, F. F. *The Epistle to the Galatians.* NIGTC. Grand Rapids: Eerdmans, 2002.

George, Timothy. *Galatians.* NAC. Nashville: B & H, 2004.

A wonderful commentary written by an accomplished church historian who shows himself an able biblical scholar.

Ryken, Philip Graham. *Galatians.* REC. Phillipsburg: P & R, 2005.

A model commentary: expositional, pastoral, confessional, and Christological.

Silva, Moisés. "Galatians." *Bible Commentary: 21ˢᵗ Century Edition.* Downers Grove: IVP, 1994. Leicester: IVP, 1994.

For exegetical assistance, see his Interpreting Galatians: Explorations in Exegetical Method, 2ⁿᵈ ed. (Grand Rapids: Baker, 2001).

Consider:

Boice, James Montgomery. *Galatians.* EBC. Grand Rapids: Zondervan, 1976.

Hansen, G. Walter. *Galatians.* IVPNT. Downers Grove: IVP, 1994. Leicester: IVP, 1994.

Luther, Martin. *Commentary on Galatians.* Grand Rapids: Baker, 1998.

Morris, Leon. *Galatians: Paul's Charter of Christian Freedom.* Downers Grove: IVP, 2003. Leicester: IVP, 2003.

Ridderbos, Herman. *St. Paul's Epistle to the Churches of Galatia.* NICNT. Grand Rapids: Eerdmans, 1976.

This has now been replaced by Ronald Y. K. Fung in this series, but Ridderbos is still to be preferred.

To be considered for sermon preparation:

Andrews, Edgar H. *Free in Christ: The message of Galatians.* WCS. Darlington: EP, 1996.

Calvin, John. *John Calvin's Sermons on Galatians.* Carlisle: BoT, 1997. Edinburgh: BoT, 1997.

Lloyd-Jones, D. Martyn. *The Cross: God's Way of Salvation.* Eastbourne: Kingsway, 1986.

Sermons on Galatians 6:14.

Sanderson, John W. *The Fruit of the Spirit.* Phillipsburg: P & R, 1999.

Stott, John R. W. *The Message of Galatians.* BST. Downers Grove: IVP, 1984. Leicester: IVP, 1984.

Thomas, Derek. *Let's Study Galatians.* Carlisle: BoT, 2004. Edinburgh: BoT, 2004.

EPHESIANS

Recommendation:

Hodge, Charles. *Ephesians.* GCS. Carlisle: BoT, 1991. Edinburgh: BoT, 1991.

Still one of the best commentaries to turn to and the most reliable guide to put into the hands of the average reader.

Lincoln, Andrew T. *Ephesians.* WBC. Waco: Word, 1990.

This is regarded as one of the best commentaries on Ephesians despite the fact that Lincoln does not think Paul wrote it! For discerning readers only, then.

O'Brien, Peter T. *The Letter to the Ephesians.* PNTC. Grand Rapids: Eerdmans, 1999. Leicester: IVP, 1999.

A masterful work. Consult before Lincoln.

Consider:

Bruce, F. F. *Colossians, Philemon, Ephesians.* NICNT. Grand Rapids: Eerdmans, 1984.

Hoehner, Harold W. *Ephesians: An Exegetical Commentary.* Grand Rapids: Baker, 2002.

Exhaustive. The most complete commentary on the Greek text.

Uprichard, Harry. *A Study Commentary on Ephesians.* EPSC. Auburn: EP, 2004. Darlington: EP, 2004.

To be considered for sermon preparation:

Calvin, John. *Sermons on Ephesians.* Carlisle: BoT, 1973. Edinburgh: BoT, 1973.

Carson, D. A. *A Call to Spiritual Reformation: Priorities from Paul and his Prayers.* Grand Rapids: Baker, 1992. Leicester: IVP, 1992.

Chapter 10, "Praying to the Sovereign God" (Ephesians 1:15-23); chapter 11, "Praying for Power" (Ephesians 3:14-21).

Ferguson, Sinclair B. *Let's Study Ephesians.* Carlisle: BoT, 2005. Edinburgh: BoT, 2005.

Ferguson, Sinclair B. *Add to your Faith.* Glasgow: Pickering and Inglis, 1980.

Chapter 9, "Fighting the Enemy."

Gurnall, William. *The Christian in Complete Armour.* 3 Volumes. Carlisle: BoT, 1990. Edinburgh: BoT, 1990.

The best on Ephesians 6.

Hughes, R. Kent. *Ephesians: The Mystery of the Body of Christ.* PWS. Wheaton: Crossway, 1990.

Olyott, Stuart. *Alive in Christ: Ephesians Simply Explained.* WCS. Darlington: EP, 1994.

Sproul, R. C. *Ephesians: The Purpose of God.* Ross-shire: CFP, 2002.

Stott, John R. W. *The Message of Ephesians.* BST. Downers Grove: IVP, 1979. Leicester: IVP, 1979.

Eight volume exposition on Ephesians by D. Martyn Lloyd Jones:

Lloyd-Jones, D. Martyn. *An Exposition of Ephesians 1:1-23: God's Ultimate Purpose.* Carlisle: BoT, 1978. Edinburgh: BoT, 1978.

Lloyd-Jones, D. Martyn. *An Exposition of Ephesians 2:1-22: God's Way of Reconciliation.* Carlisle: BoT, 1979. Edinburgh: BoT, 1979.

Lloyd-Jones, D. Martyn. *An Exposition of Ephesians 3:1-21: The Unsearchable Riches of Christ.* Carlisle: BoT, 1980.

Lloyd-Jones, D. Martyn. *An Exposition of Ephesians 4:1-16: Christian Unity.* Carlisle: BoT, 1980. Edinburgh: BoT, 1980.

Lloyd-Jones, D. Martyn. *An Exposition of Ephesians 4:17-5:17: Darkness and Light.* Carlisle: BoT, 1999. Edinburgh: BoT, 1999.

Lloyd-Jones, D. Martyn. *An Exposition of Ephesians 5:18-6:9: Life in the Spirit.* Carlisle: BoT, 1998. Edinburgh: BoT, 1998.

Lloyd-Jones, D. Martyn.*An Exposition of Ephesians 6:10-13: The Christian Warfare.* Carlisle: BoT, 1976. Edinburgh: BoT, 1976.

Lloyd-Jones, D. Martyn. *An Exposition of Ephesians 6:10-20: The Christian Solider.* Carlisle: BoT, 1977. Edinburgh: BoT, 1977.

PHILIPPIANS

Recommendation:

O'Brien, Peter T. *Philippians.* NIGNT. Grand Rapids: Eerdmans, 1991.

Silva, Moisés. *Philippians.* 2nd ed. BECNT. Grand Rapids: Baker, 2005.
Consider:

Fee, Gordon D. *Philippians.* NICNT. Grand Rapids: Eerdmans, 1995.

Müller, Jac. J. *The Epistles of Paul to the Philippians and to Philemon.* Grand Rapids: Eerdmans, 1985.

Thielman, Frank. *Philippians.* NIVAC. Grand Rapids: Zondervan, 1995.

To be considered for sermon preparation:

Bentley, Michael. *Shining in the Darkness: Philippians Simply Explained.* WCS. Darlington: EP, 1998.

Boice, James Montgomery. *Philippians.* An Expositional Commentary. Grand Rapids: Baker, 2000.

Carson, D. A. *A Call to Spiritual Reformation: Priorities from Paul and his Prayers.* Grand Rapids: Baker, 1992. Leicester: IVP, 1992.

Chapter 8, "Overcoming the Hurdles" (Philippians 1:9-11).

Ferguson, Sinclair B. *Let's Study Philippians.* Carlisle: BoT, 1997. Edinburgh: BoT, 1997.

Gwyn-Thomas, John. *Rejoice Always.* Carlisle: BoT, 1989. Edinburgh: BoT, 1989.

Sermons on Philippians 4.

Jones, Hywel R. *Philippians.* Focus on the Bible. Ross-shire: CFP, 1993.

Lloyd-Jones, D. Martyn. *The Life of Joy: A Commentary on Philippians 1 and 2.* London: Hodder & Stoughton, 1989.

Lloyd-Jones, D. Martyn. *The Life of Peace: Studies in Philippians 3 and 4.* Grand Rapids: Baker, 1992.

Maclcod, Donald. *The Humiliated and Exalted Lord.* Ed. J. Ligon Duncan III. Greenville: RAP, 1994.

On the crucial passage in chapter 2:5-13.

Motyer, J. A. *The Richness of Christ.* London: IVP, 1966.

Philip, George M. *Daily Grace from Philippians and Colossians.* Webster: EP, 2004. Darlington: EP, 2004.

COLOSSIANS

Recommendation:

Bruce, F. F. *Colossians, Philemon, Ephesians.* NICNT. Grand Rapids: Eerdmans, 1984.

O'Brien, Peter T. *Colossians, Philemon.* WBC. Waco: Word, 1982.

Consider:

Dunn, James D. G. *The Epistles to the Colossians and to Philemon.* NIGTC. Grand Rapids: Eerdmans, 1996.

A weighty text. Holds that Philemon was written by Paul but Colossians wasn't.

Lightfoot, J. B. *St. Paul's Epistles to the Colossians and to Philemon.* Peabody: Hendrickson, 1994.

Moule, H. C. G. *Studies in Colossians and Philemon.* Grand Rapids: Kregel, 1982.

Wall, Robert W. *Colossians & Philemon.* IVPNT. Downers Grove: IVP, 1993. Leicester: IVP, 1993.

Wright, N. T. *Colossians and Philemon: An Introduction and Commentary.* TNTC. Grand Rapids: Eerdmans, 1989. Leicester: IVP, 1987.

This superseded the original by H. M. Carson, but Carson is worth looking at too.

To be considered for sermon preparation:

Appéré, Guy. *The Mystery of Christ: Meditations on Colossians.* WCS. Welwyn: EP, 1984.

Bentley, Michael. *Colossians & Philemon.* The Guide. Auburn: EP, 2002. Darlington: EP, 2002.

Carson, D. A. *A Call to Spiritual Reformation: Priorities from Paul and his Prayers.* Grand Rapids: Baker, 1992. Leicester: IVP, 1992.

Chapter 6, "The Content of a Challenging Prayer" (Colossians 1:9-14).

Ferguson, Sinclair B. *A Heart for God.* Carlisle: BoT, 1987. Edinburgh: BoT, 1987.

Chapter 7, "God only Wise" (Colossians 3).

Garland, David E. *Colossians/Philemon.* NIVAC. Grand Rapids: Zondervan, 1998.

Hughes, R. Kent. *Colossians and Philemon: The Supremacy of Christ.* PWS. Wheaton: Crossway, 1989.

Lucas, R. C. *Fullness and Freedom: The Message of Colossians and Philemon.* BST. Downers Grove: IVP, 1980. Leicester: IVP, 1980.

MacArthur, John. *Colossians & Philemon.* The MacArthur New Testament Commentary. Chicago: Moody, 1992.

Philip, George M. *Daily Grace from Philippians and Colossians.* Webster: EP, 2004. Darlington: EP, 2004.

1 & 2 THESSALONIANS

Recommendation:

Green, Gene L. *The Letters to the Thessalonians.* PNTC. Grand Rapids: Eerdmans, 2002.

Wanamaker, Charles A. *The Epistles to the Thessalonians.* NIGTC. Grand Rapids: Eerdmans, 1990.

Consider:

Bruce, F. F. *1 & 2 Thessalonians.* WBC. Nashville: Thomas Nelson, 1982.

Denney, James. *The Epistles to the Thessalonians.* The Expositor's Bible. London: Hodder & Stoughton, 1899. o/p.

Marshall, I. Howard. "1 and 2 Thessalonians." *New Bible Commentary: 21st Century Edition.* Downers Grove: IVP, 1994. Leicester: IVP, 1994.

Morris, Leon. *The First and Second Epistles to the Thessalonians.* NICNT. Grand Rapids: Eerdmans, 1991.

See also his commentary in the TNTC.

To be considered for sermon preparation:

Carson, D. A. *A Call to Spiritual Reformation: Priorities from Paul and his Prayers.* Grand Rapids: Baker, 1992. Leicester: IVP, 1992.

Chapter 5, "A Passion for People" (I Thessalonians 3:9-13); chapter 2 "The Framework of Prayer" and chapter 3 "Worthy Petitions" (2 Thessalonians 1:1-12).

Holmes, Michael W. *1 & 2 Thessalonians.* NIVAC. Grand Rapids: Zondervan, 1998.

Mayhue, Richard. *1 & 2 Thessalonians: Triumphs and Trials of a Consecrated Church.* Focus on the Bible. Ross-shire: CFP, 1999.

Premillennial.

Stott, John R. W. *The Message of 1 & 2 Thessalonians.* BST. Downers Grove: IVP, 1994. Leicester: IVP, 1994.

Young, Andrew W. *Let's Study 1 & 2 Thessalonians.* Carlisle: BoT, 2001. Edinburgh: BoT, 2001.

PASTORALS

Recommendation:

Barcley, William B. *A Study Commentary on 1 and 2 Timothy.* EPSC. Auburn: EP, 2005. Darlington: EP, 2005.

Knight III, George W. *The Pastoral Epistles.* NICTC. Grand Rapids: Eerdmans, 1992.

Consider:

Fairbairn, Patrick. *Pastoral Epistles.* Minneapolis: KK, 1980.

A classic work from a Reformed Scottish perspective.

Fee, Gordon D. *1 and 2 Timothy, Titus.* NIBC. Peabody: Hendrickson, 1989.

Guthrie, Donald. *The Pastoral Epistles: An Introduction and Commentary.* TNTC. Grand Rapids: Eerdmans, 1990. Leicester: IVP, 1990.

See also his contribution in the New Bible Commentary: 21st Century Edition.

Liddon, H. P. *Explanatory Analysis of St. Paul's First Epistle to Timothy.* Minneapolis: KK, 1978.

Mounce, William D. *Pastoral Epistles.* WBC. Nashville: Thomas Nelson, 2000.

Towner, Philip H. *1-2 Timothy & Titus.* IVPNT. Downers Grove: IVP, 1994. Leicester: IVP, 1994.

To be considered for sermon preparation:

Calvin, John. *John Calvin's Sermons on Timothy and Titus.* 1579 Facsimile Edition. Carlisle: BoT, 1983. Edinburgh: BoT, 1983.

Hughes, R. Kent, and Bryan Chapell. *1 and 2 Timothy and Titus.* PWS. Wheaton: Crossway, 2000.

Knight III, George. *The Faithful Saying in the Pastoral Letters.* Grand Rapids: Baker, 1979.

Liefeld, Walter L. *1 & 2 Timothy/Titus.* NIVAC. Grand Rapids: Zondervan, 1999.

Lloyd-Jones, D. Martyn. *I Am Not Ashamed: Advice to Timothy.* London: Hodder & Stoughton, 1994.

MacArthur, John. *1 Timothy.* The MacArthur New Testament Commentary. Chicago: Moody, 1995.

MacArthur, John. *2 Timothy.* The MacArthur New Testament Commentary. Chicago: Moody, 1995.

MacArthur, John. *Titus.* The MacArthur New Testament Commentary. Chicago: Moody, 1996.

Milne, Douglas J. W. *1 & 2 Timothy & Titus.* Focus on the Bible. Rossshire: CFP, 1996.

Oden, Thomas C. *First and Second Timothy and Titus.* Interpretation Commentary. Louisville: John Knox, 1989.

Stott, John. *Guard the Truth: The Message of 1 Timothy & Titus.* BST. Downers Grove: IVP, 1996. Leicester: IVP, 1996.

Stott, John. *Guard the Gospel: The Message of 2 Timothy.* BST. Downers Grove: IVP, 1973. Leicester: IVP, 1973.

Excellent expositions!

Taylor, Thomas. *An Exposition of Titus.* Lafayette: Sovereign Grace, 1962.

A Puritan commentary.

PHILEMON

Recommendation:

Bruce, F. F. *Colossians, Philemon, Ephesians.* NICNT. Grand Rapids: Eerdmans, 1984.

O'Brien, Peter T. *Colossians, Philemon.* WBC. Nashville: Thomas Nelson, 1982.

Consider:

Dunn, James D. G. *The Epistles to the Colossians and to Philemon.* NIGTC. Grand Rapids: Eerdmans, 1996.

See comments on Colossians above.

Lightfoot, J. B. *St. Paul's Epistles to the Colossians and to Philemon.* London: MacMillian and Co., 1876. o/p.

Moule, H. C. G. *Studies in Colossians and Philemon.* Grand Rapids: Kregel, 1982.

Wall, Robert W. *Colossians & Philemon.* IVPNT. Downers Grove: IVP, 1993. Leicester: IVP, 1993.

Wright, N. T. *Colossians and Philemon: An Introduction and Commentary.* TNTC. Grand Rapids: Eerdmans, 1989. Leicester: IVP, 1987.

See comments on Colossians above.

To be considered for sermon preparation:

Bentley, Michael. *Colossians & Philemon.* The Guide. Auburn: EP, 2002. Darlington: EP, 2002.

Garland, David E. *Colossians, Philemon.* NIVAC. Grand Rapids: Zondervan, 1998.

Hughes, R. Kent. *Colossians and Philemon: The Supremacy of Christ.* PWS. Wheaton: Crossway, 1989.

Lucas, R. C. *The Message of Colossians and Philemon: Fullness and Freedom.* BST. Downers Grove: IVP, 1980. Leicester: IVP, 1980.

MacArthur, John. *Colossians & Philemon.* The MacArthur New Testament Commentary. Chicago: Moody, 1992.

Philip, George M. *Daily Grace from Philippians and Colossians.* Webster: EP, 2004. Darlington: EP, 2004.

HEBREWS

Recommendation:

Brown, John. *Hebrews.* GSC. London: BoT, 1991.

Hughes, Philip E. *A Commentary on the Epistle to the Hebrews.* Grand Rapids: Eerdmans, 1977.

Outstanding.

Lane, William. *Hebrews.* 2 Volumes. Nashville: Thomas Nelson, 1991.

Owen, John. *An Exposition of the Epistle to the Hebrews.* 7 Volumes. Carlisle: BoT, 2000. Edinburgh: BoT, 2000.

A lifetime accomplishment. One of the finest and most exhaustive expositions ever written. The story is told that upon completion Owen is said to have exclaimed, "Now my work is done; it is time for me to die!"

Consider:

Bruce, F. F. *The Epistle to the Hebrews.* NICNT. Grand Rapids: Eerdmans, 1990.

Ellingworth, Paul. *The Epistle to the Hebrews.* NIGTC. Grand Rapids: Eerdmans, 1993.

Westcott, B. F. *The Epistle to the Hebrews.* Grand Rapids: Eerdmans, 1984.

To be considered for sermon preparation:

Andrews, Edgar. *A Glorious High Throne: Hebrews Simply Explained.* WCS. Webster: EP, 2003. Darlington: EP, 2003.

Arthur, J. Philip. *No Turning Back: An exposition of the Epistle to the Hebrews.* Darlington: EP, 2003.

Brown, Raymond. *The Message of Hebrews: Christ Above All.* BST. Downers Grove: IVP, 1984. Leicester: IVP, 1984.

Guthrie, George H. *Hebrews.* NIVAC. Grand Rapids: Zondervan, 1998.

Hughes, R. Kent. *Hebrews: An Anchor for the Soul.* 2 Volumes. PWS. Wheaton: Crossway, 1993.

Jones, Hywel R. *Let's Study Hebrews.* Carlisle: BoT, 2002. Edinburgh: BoT, 2002.

Lane, William. *Call to Commitment: Responding to the Message of Hebrews.* New York: Thomas Nelson, 1985.

Stibbs, Alan M. *So Great Salvation.* Exeter: Paternoster, 1970.

Vos, Geerhardus. *The Teaching of the Epistle to the Hebrews.* Eugene, OR: Wipf & Stock, 1998.

JAMES

Recommendation:

Manton, Thomas. *James.* GSC. London: BoT, 1962.

Moo, Douglas J. *The Letter of James.* PNTC. Grand Rapids: Eerdmans, 2000.

Moo, Douglas J. *James: An Introduction and Commentary.* TNTC. Grand Rapids: Eerdmans, 1986. Leicester: IVP, 1985.

Not as thorough as his Pillar Commentary.

Consider:

Adamson, James B. *The Epistle of James.* NICNT. Grand Rapids: Eerdmans, 1995.

Davids, Peter. *The Epistle of James: A Commentary on the Greek Text.* NIGTC. Grand Rapids: Eerdmans, 1982.

Davids, Peter. *James.* NIBC. Peabody: Hendrickson, 1990.

Less technical.

Johnstone, Robert. *James.* GSC. Carlisle: BT, 1977. Edinburgh: BT, 1977.

Mayor, Joseph B. *The Epistle of St. James.* Eugene, OR: Wipf & Stock, 2003.

To be considered for sermon preparation:

Blanchard, John. *Truth for Life: A devotional commentary on the Epistle of James.* Darlington: EP, 2003.

Boice, James Montgomery. *Sure I Believe – So What?* Ross-shire: CFP, 1994.

Hughes, R. Kent. *James: Faith That Works.* PWS. Wheaton: Crossway, 1991.

Keddie, Gordon J. *The Practical Christian.* WCS. Welwyn: EP, 1989.

Motyer, Alec. *The Message of James.* BST. Downers Grove: IVP, 1998. Leicester: IVP, 1998.

Prime, Derek. *James.* Focus on the Bible. Ross-shire: CFP, 1995.

1 & 2 PETER, JUDE

Recommendation:

Bauckham, Richard J. *2 Peter and Jude.* WBC. Waco: Word, 1988.

Does not believe Peter wrote it!

Brown, John. *The First Epistle of Peter.* 2 Volumes. GSC. Carlisle: BoT, 1975. Edinburgh: BoT, 1975.

Brown, John. *Parting Counsels: 2 Peter Chapter 1.* GSC. Carlisle: BoT, 1980. Edinburgh: BoT, 1980.

Michaels, J. Ramsey. *1 Peter.* WBC. Nashville: Thomas Nelson, 1988.

Dates 1 Peter late.

Consider:

Cranfield, C. E. B. *1-2 Peter & Jude.* London: SCM, 1960.

Green, Michael. *2 Peter and Jude.* TNTC. Grand Rapids: Eerdmans, 1987. Leicester: IVP, 1987.

Grudem, Wayne. *1 Peter: An Introduction and Commentary.* TNTC. Grand Rapids: Eerdmans, 1988. Leicester: IVP, 1988.

Jobes, Karen H. *1 Peter.* BECNT. Grand Rapids: Baker, 2005.

Leighton, Robert. *Commentary on First Peter.* Grand Rapids: Kregel, 1972.

Marshall, I. Howard. *1 Peter.* IVPNT. Downers Grove: IVP, 1991. Leicester: IVP, 1991.

Moo, Douglas J. *2 Peter, Jude.* NIVAC. Grand Rapids: Zondervan, 1997.

To be considered for sermon preparation:

Adams, Thomas. *Commentary on the Second General Epistle of St. Peter.* Morgan, PA: Soli Deo Gloria, 1990.

Bentley, Michael. *Ransomed, Healed, Restored, Forgive: Learning from the Life of Peter.* Auburn: EP, 2001. Darlington: EP, 2001.

Cleave, Derek. *1 Peter.* Focus on the Bible. Ross-shire: CFP, 1999.

Clowney, Edmund P. *The Message of 1 Peter.* BST. Downers Grove: IVP, 1989. Leicester: IVP, 1994.

Donnelly, Edward. *Peter: Eyewitness of His Majesty as Disciple, Preacher, Pastor.* Carlisle: BoT, 1998. Edinburgh: BoT, 1998.

Gardner, Paul. *2 Peter & Jude.* Focus on the Bible. Ross-shire: CFP, 1999.

Harrell, William W. *Let's Study 1 Peter.* Carlisle: BoT, 2004. Edinburgh: BoT, 2004.

Lloyd-Jones, D. Martyn. *Expository Sermons on 2 Peter.* Carlisle: BoT, 1984. Edinburgh: BoT, 1984.

1-3 JOHN

Recommendation:

Candlish, Robert. *1 John.* GSC. Carlisle: BT, 1973. Edinburgh: BT, 1973.

Consider:

Bruce, F. F. *The Gospel & Epistles of John.* 2 Volumes in one. Grand Rapids: Eerdmans, 1983.

Findlay, George G. *Fellowship in Life Eternal.* Grand Rapids: Kregel, 1989.

Kruse, Colin. *The Letters of John.* PNTC. Grand Rapids: Eerdmans, 2000.

Marshall, I. Howard. *The Epistles of John.* NICNT. Grand Rapids: Eerdmans, 1973.

Stott, John. *The Letters of John: An Introduction and Commentary.* Grand Rapids: Eerdmans, 1988. Leicester: IVP, 1988.

To be considered for sermon preparation:

Barnes, Peter. *Knowing Where We Stand: The Message of John's Epistles.* WCS. Darlington: EP, 1998.

Boice, James Montgomery. *The Epistles of John. An Expositional Commentary.* Grand Rapids: Baker, 2004.

Eaton, Michael. *1, 2, & 3 John.* Focus on the Bible. Ross-shire: CFP, 1995.

Jackman, David. *The Message of John's Letters.* BST. Downers Grove: IVP, 1988. Leicester: IVP, 1988.

Lloyd-Jones, D. Martyn. *Life in Christ: Studies in 1 John.* 5 Volumes in one. Wheaton: Crossway, 2002.

<u>JUDE</u>

As above with Peter, but consider:

Benton, John. *Slandering the Angels: The message of Jude.* WCS. Darlington: EP, 1999.

Lawlor, George Lawrence. *The Epistle of Jude.* Biblical and Theological Studies. Nutley: P & R, 1972.

Jenkyn, William. *Exposition of the Epistle of Jude.* Minneapolis: James & Klock, 1976.

Manton, Thomas. *Jude.* GSC. Carlisle: BoT, 1989. Edinburgh: BoT, 1989.

REVELATION

Recommendation:

Beale, G. K. *The Book of Revelation.* NIGTC. Grand Rapids: Eerdmans, 1998.

A monumental and comprehensive work. Amillennial.

Hendriksen, William. *More Than Conquerors: An Interpretation of the Book of Revelation.* Grand Rapids: Baker, 1998.

Very accessible and readable. The opening section is crucial reading for interpreting apocalyptic literature. Amillennial.

Consider:

Chilton, David. *Days of Vengeance: Exposition of the Book of Revelation.* Forth Worth: Dominion Press, 1987.

A (unique!) postmillennial interpretation. Chilton's analysis of Revelation is, quite frankly, weird. But he has some good insights here and there. As an RTS graduate, he deserves to be read.

Hoekema, Anthony, *The Bible and the Future.* Grand Rapids: Eerdmans, 1994.

Though not a commentary, essential reading for the Amillennial position. See also Cornelis P. Venema, The Promise of the Future (Edinburgh: BoT, 2000).

Hughes, P. E. *The Book of Revelation: A Commentary.* Grand Rapids: Eerdmans, 1990. Leicester: IVP, 1990.

Morris, Leon. *Revelation: An Introduction and Commentary.* TNTC. Grand Rapids: Eerdmans, 1987. Leicester: IVP, 1987.

Mounce, Robert H. *The Book of Revelation.* NICNT. Grand Rapids: Eerdmans, 1977.

Non-dispensational premillennial.

Murray, Beasley. "Revelation." *New Bible Commentary: 21ˢᵗ Century Edition.* Downers Grove: IVP, 1994. Leicester: IVP, 1994.

Osborne, Grant R. *Revelation.* BECNT. Grand Rapids: Baker, 2002.

Swete, H. B. *Commentary on Revelation.* Grand Rapids: Kregel, 1977.

To be considered for sermon preparation:

Brooks, Richard. *The Lamb is All the Glory.* WCS. Welwyn: EP, 1986.

Fortner, Don. *Discovering Christ in Revelation.* Auburn: EP, 2002. Darlington: EP, 2002.

Gardner, Paul. *Revelation: The Compassion and Protection of Christ.* Focus on the Bible. Ross-shire: CFP, 2001.

Johnson, Dennis E. *Triumph of the Lamb: A Commentary on Revelation.* Phillipsburg: P & R, 2001.

Poythress, Vern S. *The Returning King: A Guide to the Book of Revelation.* Phillipsburg: P & R, 2000.

Thomas, Derek. *Let's Study Revelation.* Carlisle: BoT, 2003. Edinburgh: BoT, 2003.

Wilcock, Michael. *I Saw Heaven Opened.* BST. Downers Grove: IVP, 1975. Leicester: IVP, 1975.

For further study on eschatology:

Bock, Darrell L., ed. *Three Views on the Millennium and Beyond.* Grand Rapids: Zondervan, 1999.

Craig Blaising – Premillennialism. Kenneth Gentry – Postmillennialism, and Robert Strimple – Amillennialism.

Pate, C. Marvin, ed. *Four Views on the Book of Revelation.* Grand Rapids: Zondervan, 1998.

Kenneth Gentry – Preterist. Sam Hamstra – Idealist, C. Marvin Pate – Progressive Dispensationalist, and Robert Thomas – Classical Dispensationalist.

APPENDIX:

ESSENTIAL SYSTEMATIC THEOLOGY TEXTS FOR A PREACHER'S LIBRARY

Below is a selection of important one volume and multi-volume theology texts. Most are from a reformed and evangelical persuasion but not all. Like the commentaries, this list is by no means exhaustive. This appendix is included because of the belief that preachers should not only be able and articulate expositors but also capable and competent systematicians. The Bible needs to be read and proclaimed in its parts and as a coherent and unified whole. Therefore, exegesis and systematics are necessary for rightly dividing the word. If you are operating on a tight budget, Calvin, Berkhof, and Murray are musts!

ONE VOLUME SYSTEMATIC THEOLOGY TEXTS

Recommendation:

Berkhof, Louis. *Systematic Theology.* Grand Rapids: Eerdmans, 1996.

> *Though over seventy years old, Berkhof is still the best one volume systematic theology. For your one stop theological resource, this is your book. Berkhof was professor at Calvin Theological Seminary and writes from a Dutch Reformed perspective. Edited by R. Muller, this volume combines Berkhof's work on prolegomena which serves as an introduction to his systematic.*

Grudem, Wayne. *Systematic Theology.* Grand Rapids: Zondervan, 2000.

Grudem is a professor at Phoenix Seminary and writes theology the way it should be written – dogmatically, devotionally, and doxologically. He writes from a reformed and evangelical Baptist perspective. A helpful section on spiritual warfare (a topic which few systematic theologies tackle!). Takes a non-cessationist approach to gifts and a historic pre-millennial view of eschatology.

Hodge, A. A. *Outlines of Theology.* Carlisle: BoT, 1999. Edinburgh: BoT, 1999.

Son of the great Charles Hodge, this volume was written for students and laymen. This is a classic work and good introduction to the Princetonians. For those not eager to plod through the three volumes of his father but want a taste of Princeton theology, this is your resource. Follows a question and answer format.

Macleod, Donald. *A Faith to Live By.* Ross-shire: CFP, 1998.

If the study of theology is new territory for you, you may want to start here. Professor Macleod is the Principal at the Free Church College in Edinburgh, Scotland. His work is clear, straightforward, and devotional. He writes from a reformed and Presbyterian perspective. Great introduction to covenant theology. His discussion on creation will provoke thought.

Packer, James I. *Concise Theology.* Wheaton: Tyndale House, 1993.

Board of Governors' Professor of Theology at Regent College, Packer is one of the leading evangelical voices of our day. This volume is an excellent introduction to the field of theology. Packer has an economy of words and ability to express complex truth in a 'concise' manner that few have. With each chapter only a few pages long, this is a great place to start. An articulate and accessible work.

Reymond, Robert L. *A New Systematic Theology of the Christian Faith.* 2nd ed. Nashville: Thomas Nelson, 1998.

> *As a new contribution to the field of systematics, he deals with contemporary issues not dealt with by earlier systematicians (e.g. – Open Theism) but neglects others (e.g. – liberation theology and feminist theology). Essential reading, despite some idiosyncrasies, particularly in his development of the doctrine of the trinity in relation to historic creeds and confessions as well as his discussion of the nature of univocal/analogical knowledge. He writes from a reformed and Presbyterian perspective.*

Westminster Confession of Faith. Glasgow: Free Presbyterian Publications, 2001.

> *Though not a systematic theology, the Westminster Confession of Faith still represents the clearest and most concise statement of reformed theology. As Warfield famously stated, "The Westminster Standards are the richest and most precise and best guarded statement ever penned of all that enters into evangelical religion." A preacher would do well to master its contents. This edition also includes The Larger and Shorter Catechism, The Sum of Saving Knowledge, The Directory for the Public Worship of God, and other important and worthy documents. Also, keep an eye on the developing Westminster Assembly Project and the four volume edited series by J. Ligon Duncan, III entitled The Westminster Confession into the 21st Century (Ross-shire: CFP, 2003-). Baptists may also want to consult the London Confession of 1689.*

Consider:

Ames, William. *Marrow of Modern Divinity*. Grand Rapids: Baker, 1997.

A student of the great William Perkins, Ames was one of the most important Puritans of the early seventeenth century. Saw theology as "the doctrine of living to God." Experiential Calvinism at its best.

Boice, James Montgomery. *Foundations of the Christian Faith*. Downers Grove: IVP, 1986. Leicester: IVP, 1986.

Boice follows a similar structure to Calvin's Institutes. Each chapter was originally delivered as a sermon at Tenth Presbyterian; therefore, its homiletic style lends itself to good devotional reading. A sterling example of how to preach and apply theology.

Boyce, James P. *Abstract of Systematic Theology*. Phillipsburg: P & R, 1996.

Boyce was the first president of Southern Baptist Theological Seminary and was an ardent Calvinist. This has been a standard text for reformed Baptists.

Dabney, Robert L. *Systematic Theology*. Carlisle: BoT, 2002. Edinburgh: BoT, 2002.

Dabney is considered by many, including Warfield, to be the finest of all the American Southern Presbyterians. Dabney was Professor of Systematic and Polemic Theology at Union Theology Seminary in Virginia. The only complete systematic from a 19th century American Southern Presbyterian perspective.

Erickson, Millard. *Christian Theology*. 2nd ed. Grand Rapids: Baker, 1998.

An evangelical theologian who currently teaches at Western Seminary. He interacts with many contemporary issues in theology.

Heppe, Heinrich. ***Reformed Dogmatics: Set Out and Illustrated from the Sources.*** Grand Rapids: Baker Books, 1978.

A marvelous assortment of the best quotations from the Reformed Scholastics on a wide array of theological topics.

McGrath, Alister E. ***Christian Theology: An Introduction.*** 2nd ed. Oxford: Blackwell, 1997.

Principal of Wycliffe Hall, Oxford, McGrath surveys the history and development of theology, but his volume is just that – a survey – and is not a systematic theology. If you are looking for constructive, positive theology, you will be left wanting. But for a descriptive introduction to key figures and ideas, this volume may help. There is also a companion reader entitled The Christian Theology Reader (Oxford: Blackwell, 1995).

Shedd, William G. T. ***Dogmatic Theology.*** 3rd ed. Phillisburg: P&R, 2003.

Now in one, unabridged volume! Alan Gomes is to be applauded for a fine job at editing and annotating this classic text. Shedd taught at Union Theological Seminary in New York in the late 19th century and was a staunch Calvinist. Comprehensive in scope.

Sproul, R. C. ***Essential Truths of the Christian Faith.*** Wheaton: Tyndale House, 1992.

Similar to Packer's Concise Theology, Sproul is one of the most popular reformed leaders of the day. This is an excellent introduction to theology and ideal for a small study group.

Strong, Augustus H. *Systematic Theology.* Philadelphia: Judson Press, 1943.

Professor of Rochester Theological Seminary in New York in the nineteenth century, Strong was a moderately reformed Northern Baptist whose volume was a long time standard only to be replaced by Erickson. Tended towards Amyraldianism.

Van Til, Cornelius. *An Introduction to Systematic Theology.* Phillipsburg: P & R, 1992.

This is not a full systematic, but Van Til provides fascinating discussions on the doctrines of Scripture, God, and epistemology. His work, though at times muddied, is crucial for understanding presuppositional apologetics.

MULTI-VOLUME SYSTEMATIC THEOLOGY TEXTS

Recommendation:

Calvin, John. *Institutes of the Christian Religion.* 2 Volumes. Philadelphia: Westminster/John Knox Press, 1993.

What can be said about this work? No work in theology has had greater influence on the western world than Calvin's Institutes (make sure and get the McNeill and Battles edition). Following the general pattern of the Apostle's Creed, the Institutes is a compendium of theological truth. But this is no stale theology. Calvin wrote a 'sum of piety' to encourage and instruct fellow Frenchmen who were being persecuted (and even martyred) for their faith! If you have never read Calvin, you may want to start with Book III, for his explanation of the sum of the Christian Life is one of the finest examples of devotional literature ever written.

Edwards, Jonathan. *The Works of Jonathan Edwards.* 2 Volumes. Carlisle: BoT, 1985. Edinburgh: BoT, 1985.

Though he never wrote a complete systematic, his writings covered a wide range of the standard loci. Affectionate theology at its very best. For those interested in Edwards' study, the pricy but outstanding Yale edition is worthy of consideration.

Hodge, Charles. *Systematic Theology.* 3 Volumes. USA: Henrickson, 2001.

Hodge was professor of systematic theology at Princeton Theological Seminary before Warfield. This magnum opus was the result of an unprecedented fifty year teaching career. Hodge's work has long been considered one of the standard texts of reformed theology. *His opening chapter on theological method and articulation of theology as science is essential for understanding the intellectual milieu of 19th century theology.*

Murray, John. *Collected Writings of John Murray.* 4 Volumes. Carlisle: BoT, 2001. Edinburgh: BoT, 2001.

If you already have Calvin, your next purchase needs to be Murray's works. Taught at Westminster Theological Seminary during the mid-twentieth century, these volumes are a collection of Murray's articles, lectures, and works. Murray never wrote a complete systematic, but one wishes he had! He had a facility with communicating rich biblical and theological truth in a clear and cogent manner. Some may disagree with his articulation of the Adamic Administration and covenant theology. Nevertheless, read and re-read John Murray.

Warfield, Benjamin B. *The Works of Benjamin B. Warfield.* 10 Volumes. Grand Rapids: Baker, 2000.

Beyond his work on the inspiration and authority of Scripture, Warfield has not received the recognition he is due. Warfield was professor of Didactic and Polemic Theology at Princeton Seminary for the last part of the nineteenth and first part of the twentieth century. Though his works are not a complete systematic theology, they are a rich resource of exegetical, historical, and systematic theology. See especially his works on Christology, Calvin and Calvinism, and the Westminster Assembly. Few in America have matched his theological astuteness.

Consider:

Bavinck, Herman. *Reformed Dogmatics: Prolegomena.* Grand Rapids: Baker, 2003.

Bavinck, Herman. *Reformed Dogmatics: God and Creation.* Grand Rapids: Baker, 2004.

Volumes 3 and 4 are pending. The Dutch Reformed Translation Society is to be commended for their translation of Bavinck's work. Though his volume on the doctrine of God has been in English for years, the translation of the rest of his work on dogmatics will serve as a valuable contribution to the study of systematic theology. He writes from a Dutch Reformed perspective.

Berkouwer, G. C. *Studies in Dogmatics.* 12 Volumes. Grand Rapids: Eerdmans, 1961.

Modified reformed theology from a Dutch perspective. Tends toward neo- orthodoxy.

Bloesch, Donald G. *Christian Foundations.* 7 Volumes. Downers: Grove: IVP, 1992-2004.

Emeritus Professor of Theology at Dubuque Theological Seminary. Redefines classical view of the inerrancy and authority of Scripture in the name of the Reformed tradition. Defends a trans-millennialism and generally conservative neo-orthodox.

Cunnigham, William. *Historical Theology.* 2 Volumes. Carlisle: BoT, 1994. Edinburgh: BoT, 1994.

Cunningham was perhaps Scotland's greatest theologian. He was a contemporary of Hodge and the Principal of New College, Edinburgh where he also held the chair of Church History. Though this work is entitled Historical Theology, it is a rich source of systematic theology. John Macleod once said "this magnum opus will remain as a masterpiece in the field of historical theology in which from the standpoint of a loyal acceptance of consistent Reformed teaching he passes the thinking of the Christian centuries under review."

Muller, Richard. ***Post-Reformation Reformed Dogmatics.*** 4 Volumes. Grand Rapids: Baker, 2002.

> *This is historical theology at its best. For the past twenty five years, Muller, professor at Calvin Theological Seminary, has steadily worked to diffuse the myth of the alleged Calvin and Calvinists dichotomy. Only covers Prolegomena, Scripture, the essence and attributes of God, and the Trinity. Heavy reading.*

Turretin, Francis. ***Institutes of Elenctic Theology.*** 3 Volumes. Translated by G. M. Giger. Edited by J. T. Dennison, Jr. Phillipsburg: P & R, 1997.

> *Turretin taught at the Academy of Geneva and represents the choicest of Post-Reformation scholasticism. His massive work was the textbook, along with Calvin, used by Hodge, Dabney, and many others. Arguably, the best Systematic Theology ever written.*